Notes To My Kids:

Little Stories About My Grown Up Kids

By

Jeffery W. Turner

Copyright 2013 © Jeffery W. Turner

All rights reserved. No part of this publication may be reproduced or transmitted in any form or by any means, electronic or mechanical, including photocopy, recording, or any information storage and retrieval system, without permission in writing from the publisher.

Published in the USA

ISBN - 0-615-77860-7

ISBN - 978-0-615-77860-0

Also by Jeffery W. Turner:

Notes to Stephanie: Middle Aged Love Letters and Life Stories

Notes to Stephanie: Days Remembered

Table of Contents

Foreword 9
Roger's Premature Birth 12
Jane's Easier Birth...17
Baby Roger and I at the Park 22
Baby Jane Naps with Dad 25
Bath Time and Bedtime Stories 28
Home with Baby Jane 33
Baby Roger in the NICU..36
Roger Barfs in the Car...41
Sebastian the Crab..44
Dad's Diabetes 49
Going Strolling with Roger and Jane.....................52
Mom and Dad Have Food Poisoning....................56
Roger Didn't Sleep for a Year 59
MeeMaw and Granddad Tom 62
Grandmama and Granddad Harry 65
Xmas and Audiology with Roger...........................70
MeeMaw's Cooking...73
Granddad Harry's Spaghetti..................................77

Granddad Tom's Smoker	80
Your Rooms at My House	84
Bricks with your Names on Them	87
Jane Walks Early	90
Roger Goes Potty	92
Watching Disney, Barney, and 'Toons	95
An Autographed Pizza Box	98
Dr. Scroggie	101
Mrs. Travis at Sycamore School	104
The New Park	107
At the Fort Worth Zoo	111
Feeding the Fish Pennies	114
Jane at Fall Creek	117
Watching Mr. Hawk, Mr. Roadrunner, the Buzzards, and the Donkeys	120
Seeing You Each Week	126
Your Nicknames	131
The Actress Named Jane	134
Granddad Tom Dies	137
Granddad Harry Dies	144
MeeMaw and Granddad's House	148
Easter Egg Hunts with The Calhouns	153

Xmas with Me 157
Xmas with MeeMaw 161
One Xmas at Granbury...164
Watching Cartoons with Roger..............................167
Swimming in my Pool...171
Wolf Calling in Fort Worth......................................175
The Aliens at Aurora...178
My Recipes for You...182
Your Christenings 185
You Babysitters...189
Christmas at Grandmama's and Granddad Harry's...193
Swimming at Grandmama's....................................196
Working at the Rent Houses 199
Jess and Madge..203
Your Friend Curtis 209
Al and Anita and Branford, Too 212
Tom and Carol..216
Seeing Harold Taft 221
Swing Sets and a Tree House.................................225
The House on Monterrey 228
Gifts You Gave Me..231

My Cheap Xmas Trees 234
Your Pets 237
Making You Stuff 241
Lullabies 246
Fever and the Bathtub 250
Riding Segways in Austin 254
Seeing Owen Roane 258
Eating at Wyatt's Cafeteria 263
Learning to Drive Cars 267
Breakfast with Roger on The Way to
    Sycamore School 271
Roger and Terms Of Endearment 274
Fire Escape Plans 277
Cutting through the Country 280
Uncle Mike Dies 283
The Turner Extended Family 287
Birthday Cakes I Should Not Have Baked 291
Roger's PT and OT 295
Country Day School 298
PSE, Marsha, and Roger 302
Playing Sports 306
Feeding You Solid Food 309

Jane the Geologist	313
Roger the Rifleman	317
Trick or Treat with an Assault Rifle	320
A Baby Doll for Jane	324
Time's a Funny Thing	328
Afterward	334
Thanks To & Pictures	336
For More Information	337

Foreword

After writing and successfully publishing the two *Notes to Stephanie* (*NTS*) books, I asked myself: "What next?" After some thought, I decided to write two more books about my family, using the same general format as the first two books, but with many new and funny stories that were left untold after the first two books.

This book is a collection of stories about my two children mentioned in the two *NTS* books. The other will be about things that happened before my children were born. In short they would be, as is *Days Remembered*, a memoir of sorts, whose events are finally told in print. The compilation will be called *The Notes Series*.

This format works wells for me as a writer but also works well for the reader. The notes are short and to the point. Each note is both independent; readers can read it in one sitting, and convenient; or several.

As in *Days Remembered,* I have not assigned dates to the notes since so many of the stories happened as long as 27 years ago. Regardless, these are things that were important, funny, or milestones in the lives of my two children.

As in the first two books, I have not used my children's real names. They are simply called "Jane" and "Roger" again. While these and other names are not real, the stories are true, although some of the details have faded with time.

Hopefully, these little tales of kids now grown will remind you of things your children did when they were growing up and making that long journey from child to young adult. My hope is that you see a glimpse of children's lives, as I did, from the perspective of someone who enjoyed the happy times, worried when things were tough, and in the end, witnessed the silhouette of beauty and luster of magic of children growing up… finding their own path.

Jeff Turner, 1/1/2012.

Jeffery W. Turner

Roger's Premature Birth

To Roger:

By far, the day that everyone remembers the most, was the day you were born. Most babies are born normally with no complications. Your birth was not. You were born three months early, due to your mom's acute toxemia.

Until your mom got the toxemia, her pregnancy was normal, and nothing seemed wrong. But one day, she was swollen and did not feel good. When I worked at Arthur Andersen, I remember she came to downtown Fort Worth to eat lunch with me, and she did not look right. That was on a Friday afternoon; that Saturday evening, we went to Harris Hospital.

Her blood pressure was extremely high, and the doctors were concerned she might have a stroke. Many women get toxemia, but few get it as bad as she did. After much anxiety filled discussion, the doctors decided that the baby (we did not yet know you were a boy), had to be delivered---to save both of you.

Your mom was pretty much out of it and did not know what was going on. Your grandparents were there, and I was beyond worried; but I stayed calm as I always do in such times. Surgery was scheduled, and an emergency "c-section" was performed at 1:00 p.m. on January 27, 1985.

The family sat nervously, gritting their teeth, after they took your mom to the operating room. What was not a long time seemed like forever as we sat in the surgical waiting room. The doctor eventually came into the waiting room and said your mom was fine and that the baby, a boy, was delivered and was now resting in the neonatal intensive care unit. I was calm, but not everyone else. I recall seeing my dad in tears. It was the first time I had ever seen him cry in my life. Granddad Harry, a Catholic, wanted a priest to give you last rights because it was feared you might die. It was not a fun day for those who awaited your entry into the world. But it really made me grow up. You did not die, and now, you are a hardworking grown man. For both, I am grateful.

What made me burst into tears, finally, was the sight of you for the first time. I knew you were little (two and one half pounds to be precise), but I did not realize how small you were until I saw you through a crack in the curtains. I saw you lying there, small enough to fit in my hand, hooked up to wires and tubes, and wrapped in blankets to keep you warm. It made me seize up like an overheated motor and I gritted my teeth, went to my knees, and I cried. No one saw me. The stress and shock of what happened finally became real.

Dealing with all of this did not get any easier. They operated the next day to close your PDA (patent ductus arteriosus is a "hole in your heart"). It prevented your respiratory system from functioning properly. When a baby comes into the world full term, it closes by itself when breathing begins after the birth. Since you were early, that did not happen, so it had to be done with surgery—open heart surgery. The scar is still around your left side today—and every time I saw you as a boy, without a shirt, I was reminded of that day; that long day, that difficult day, that beautiful day.

The operation was hastily scheduled and they took you into the OR. The family sat around with gritted teeth again. The surgeon finally came out and said the procedure was successful, and you were okay. We were relieved that you had made it through well and had a chance to get better and one day go home.

In the end, the day you were born was more of an event than most. It was traumatic, stressful, and wonderful in the end. You made it into the world, albeit not easily. Few young children have to go through such things, but this trial made me mature very fast and made me focus my attention on things larger than me. You.

The stage was set for the struggle that was to come. For three difficult months, you were a resident of Harris Hospital. But that long road is a story that I will tell later. Your birth was miraculous enough for one memorable day and for this note. I will never forget it, for sure.

Jane's Easier Birth

To Jane:

After Roger's very traumatic birth, yours was mostly uneventful. Certainly a "tale of two babies," if you will, a fascinating set of contrasts played out at Harris Hospital.

Your mom's pregnancy was not without its own drama. We were very scared when your mom had to have an amniocentesis, a test of fluid in the womb. Another test, the Alpha-Fetoprotein check, said it might be possible that you had Down's Syndrome. I was very much aware of this condition since one of my aunts, Granddad Tom's sister Sue, had Down's. As a result, the test was scheduled, nervously.

The test was pretty intense for everyone. The doctor pulled out a long needle and readied to plunge it into your mom's big belly to extract the amniotic fluid that was required. Your mom gripped my hand tightly. I was in shock and she was scared—and awake during the whole thing. I clearly recall the huge needle that looked like it was a foot long as they stuck it into her belly. The doctor stuck it in, and your mom had a wild and wide-eyed look on her face, but never cried out. I feared they might shish-kabob *you* with that thing that resembled a hunting spear, not a needle. The fluid came out and mercifully the procedure was over.

Then we waited and shivered. After a few days, the results came back. Normal. Whew! We were more than relieved, to say the least, since our minds were filled with the memories of how your brother came into this world. What else could go wrong?

Well, something did in the last trimester. Your mom got toxemia again, like she had with Roger. Your mom and I, plus your grandparents (Granddad Harry had just died before that), were petrified. Thankfully, this bout of toxemia was much milder than she had with your brother.

To lessen the risk of another premature birth, the doctor prescribed a reduced schedule for your mom.

She had to stay in bed and not work to reduce the stress on her body. With her resting, we counted down the days until your birth. Your mom had to have a scheduled "c-section" due to the problems she had with Roger. We knew almost to the minute when you would be born.

And the day came. We went to Harris Hospital early in the morning and the staff began preparations. Your mom was awake during the entire procedure. They wheeled her into the delivery room, and the doctors and nurses began. I was there, too, but in a lot of pain with a ruptured disk. Every move I made hurt like hell, but you and your mom were the priority. I would return to Harris not long after your birth for back surgery; but back to you and your mom.

They gave your mom a local anesthesia and then something stronger. Then it got weird. The doctor got out a scalpel out and started slicing away on your mom's belly. We watched with our eyes bugged-out. He started to cut, and then with tongs, he removed a huge piece of your mom's belly skin and tissue to start the incision – it looked like fatty bacon and it wiggled as it was withdrawn. That got my attention, but thankfully no nausea. He kept working away, and it was not long until you literally popped straight up out of mom, where I could see your little face covered with goo and blood. The doctor pulled you out, the umbilical cord trailing from your tummy and back into your mom. Your mom was awake all of this time and did not say much. She did talk to the doc when he asked her questions. But when she saw you, she smiled and grinned, even with the strain of the traumatic event. I was okay, too. I know I smiled; I couldn't stop it. The nurses kept asking me if I was okay. I guess they thought I might faint.

But I did not get sick or pass out; I kept my gaze on you and your mom. You started crying, and they quickly cleaned you up. The umbilical cord was cut, and they wrapped you up in a blanket; your mom held you first. Then I got to hold you – there you were, our little girl, safe and sound with nothing wrong.

And so it was that day in the delivery room at Harris. A mostly routine birth if you can call seeing someone slice up your wife something routine. Regardless of the sight of blood and other hospital gore, it was a happy day. You were safely born, your mom was okay, and our lives went on. Time has passed, but I still remember everything fondly, the day you popped out of your mom's belly, so quickly, so happy and so healthy. We smiled then and haven't stopped yet.

Baby Roger at the Park

To Roger:

One warm spring day after you were born and finally home, I put you in your blue stroller and pushed you down Sandy Lane to the Old Park. That day was like so many that time of the year. It was warm and sunny with a few fluffy white clouds streaming to the north on the south breeze. It was a perfect day to be in the park with you when you were little.

What I remember the most about that afternoon, a Saturday I think, was holding you against me on a swing. We went back and forth many times, and you fell asleep against my chest. You were out like a light, as I faced north to the other side of the park, where I could see the fence of our back yard with the big oak tree towering over the roof of our house on Monterrey Drive. It was a view of our little part of the world from what became a favorite place for you and your sister.

As I looked at our house, I kept swinging slowly with you. There was no one around, and the park was quiet and still. The birds were chirping above our heads, and the wind swooshed through big oak trees. Except for the brief sound of a car on Sandy Lane, everything was calm and serene.

And that instance of quiet, the all-surrounding silence, was most clear that day—a time of calm after the chaos of your birth. There you were, my little boy, sound asleep in my arms. You, who had been so very sick, were now home and well with your dad, who loved you so very much.

That time was very special to me. You seemed to know you were safe and sound as you slept soundly up against me on that swing in the Old Park near our former home. I'll never forget that moment—an instant of peace when I thought back about the terrible time you had been through not so long before. We all go through awful times of peril, fear and turmoil and they eventually transition back to great calming moments of safety, tranquility and quiet. That peaceful, warm spring day was one of those great days.

Baby Jane Naps

To Jane:

Not long after you were born, I had back surgery. When you were born, I was in a lot of pain. It was something I had endured for months. In fact, the day before my surgery, I hurt so much I could not get up off the floor on my own. Granddad Tom had to pick me up while I screamed out loud. I was in very bad shape. Then blessedly, I had the surgery, which went well, and my pain was gone. The sharp aches and bolt-like throbs that went down my legs had ceased, but I had to stay home from work for six weeks and not get up much. Hence, I was on the couch or in bed a lot. But that was okay, as you will see.

Since you were a newborn, your mom was home. MeeMaw was there, too, helping us out because I could not. Your room was upstairs, but I was not allowed to go up there; so I could not tend to you in the middle of the night. When you woke up, I could hear you cry, while your mom or MeeMaw got up to get you a bottle or change you. I was stuck downstairs in the guest bedroom, helpless to help.

But during the day, you **were** downstairs, and I did pitch in. Even though I could not sit up much, I still held and fed you. Since you were a good baby and not too fussy, you were easy to tend to. I still see that in your disposition today; so happy and so loving.

Back to holding you as a newborn: one clear and powerful memory I have is when I was back on the bed after lunch one day. You had been fed, and MeeMaw brought you into me. She said something simple like, "here is your daughter, and she needs a nap". She was bringing me a great and valuable gift – you, of course. Indeed, you were a great and tiny treasure that I loved having near me. Your grandmother laid you down on my right side, wrapped up in a warm blanket, and went back in the den with your mom.

Turning slowly on my side (I was not supposed to move fast or jerk about), I cuddled you up close. Your thin, brown hair curled around your little head, you breathed softly and slept. I was tired and soon fell asleep on that late March day.

These things happened several times when I was home during that time. Being a good and loving dad, I always wanted to be part of your life—and I did the same thing with Roger. Holding you close on the bed helped build our parent to child bond. Napping with you was a small part of that natural flow.

A little thing like a nap can go a long way to bring a father and child closer without either of them knowing it at the time. Now that you are grown, it is still one my most wonderful memories of you. I wish I could forget the horrible back pain but without that surgery and recovery, I wouldn't be telling you this tale. Realizing that, you can see that something bad in my life gave birth to something good—this story and my precious memories of you.

Jeffery W. Turner

Bath Time and Bed Time

To Roger and Jane:

Baths

When children are little, mom and dad have to do some things for you. Bathing is one of those activities, as is getting you ready for bed each night. Like most couples who work all day, we did those things with you every night.

The process was the same each night. Fill up the bathtub with warm water, get you undressed, put you in the tub, and throw in a gaggle of bathtub toys. Then soap and shampoo came out, and sometimes you both hated those. You were scrubbed, and your hair rinsed out to get rid of the dirt and grime you had collected that day.

Then it was play time in the water, which was one of your favorite things. We had a ton of bath toys in your bathroom upstairs—rubber ducks, fish, boats, and

Little Mermaid things, too. They would all go in the tub, and you would splash away until the water got too cool. Sometimes, you splashed too hard, and water flew out of the tub onto the floor, which would be soaked up with a towel. That was work cleaning up, but it was just a part of the day and things kids do.

Three of the bathroom items I remember (even now) were a yellow rubber duck, Sudley's Shower, and Obie.

The rubber duck was nothing unique, but it was something you both played with. I want to say at one point years back, you still had it at your mom's house.

Obie, also known as "Bug Out Bob", was a squeeze toy, shaped like a bowling pin whose eyes, ears, and nose popped out when you squeezed him hard. Your mom and I would grab him and make some noise, like we were in great pain. You kids would laugh at this, and we would do it over and over again, and then you would laugh some more.

Now Sudley was a plastic elephant head that fit over the shower faucet and supposedly amused the child using it in the tub. It was grayish blue and had a hose with a shower head attached for its snout. I do not remember what prompted us to buy it or if it was a gift, but Roger liked it most. What is funny is that you can still buy a Sudley and an Obie on the web today.

Bed

When the playing was done and the water had turned cold, we would pluck you gently out of the tub and dry you off. We put on your pajamas and dried your hair. When it was cold, you both wore pajamas with feet on them to keep you warm—"footies" they were called.

Once you were dressed, it was story time. Story time was fun but its purpose was to get you tired and ready for bed. Like most families, we had a bunch of children's books. There were the usual titles by authors like Dr. Seuss and the like. But the one that stands out the most after all of these years was

Goodnight Moon by Margaret Wise Brown. It was a fine, little book with soft pastel colors and read with a soothing, gentle cadence. I can still hear myself reading it in my mind with one of you on my lap. "**Goodnight moon,**" I would quietly say.

After reading books in the rocking chair, it was time for your crib or bed. I would put the book down and gently lay you down. You might still be awake, but I always kissed you good night, told you to sleep tight and have sweet dreams, and told you I loved you. I would cover you up, turn off your light, close your bedroom door, and go downstairs to finish the day with your mom.

That continued until you were each old enough to bathe and dress yourselves. While I think Sudley is gone, your mom still has *Goodnight Moon* at her house. So one day when you have your own kids, get your own copy of *Goodnight Moon*—it is still in print— and read it's quiet, comforting words at the end of the day. When your own kids are on your lap listening to you read, picture you on my lap falling asleep in your warm "footies" by your bed. And maybe a new Sudley and Obie, plus a replacement rubber ducky, will be in the bathroom nearby, ready for the next night's bath.

Home with Baby Jane

To Jane:

One day when we were alone at the Monterrey house, I was playing with you. You were maybe six months old. Your mom and Roger were out, and we had the run of the place.

You were a very good baby. You smiled big and were not fussy unless you were sick or needed changing. However, on that day you were not as happy as usual. I do not remember why, but you were not in a good mood.

I remember sitting you up on the kitchen countertop—you were old enough to sit upright on your own. While I retrieved something for you, you cried, loud and continuously. You were not happy and were, for once, demanding.

At that point, I did something I seldom ever did. I snapped at you, telling you to stop crying. Being someone who is patient and not prone to anger, I am not sure why I did that; but it made you cry even more. You had a look of hurt and confusion on your little face, which normally had a smile. "Why did you do that, Daddy?" your face spoke to me without words.

Realizing what I had done, I immediately rushed to you and picked you up, holding you tight in my arms. I told you I was sorry many times, and I even cried because I had obviously hurt you so. I felt about two inches high. Your tears tore me apart. I had done you wrong, and I needed to let you know I loved you so.

After a short time, you stopped crying. I looked at you and told you I was sorry and that I loved you. I hugged you tight, and you were okay. You calmed down and smiled at me again like you always did before. You seemed to tell me, "Now that's how you normally act, Daddy." That little smile from you, my little baby girl, let me know something important that day. A big hug and a word of love can do much to wipe away the tears of sickness and hurt. It is something we should always remember before we snap or snarl at someone we love dearly. Love goes a lot further in life than anger.

Baby Roger in the NICU

To Roger:

After your birth, you stayed in the neonatal intensive care unit (the NICU) at Harris; your home for the first three months of your life. It felt like your mom and I lived there, too. We were there almost all the time with you.

Each day, we came to see you. Your mom was there while I worked. On my lunch break, I would go over to see you and return after work to sit with your mom by the side of your crib. You were on a ventilator and hooked up to many wires, which recorded your vital signs.

After a point, we were allowed to pick you up and hold you, which was a major event and it wasn't routine. The first step was doing an operating-room-like scrub. We had to wash our hands and arms a certain way. Then we donned medical scrubs. Finally, we would sit down in one of the many rocking chairs, and a nurse handed you to your mom and me and our waiting arms. It was a wonderful thing, and yet, it was something scary. At first, I thought we might hurt you because you were so small. The sensor alarms would go off if we moved wrong—we had to be careful when you were in our arms. But like most difficult things, we overcame the fear, and it finally became routine, if there is such a thing in that state.

We fed you while still sitting in one of the rocking chairs by the cribs. The nurses would come by and watch us and check your sensors showing your pulse, respiration rate, and the ever-important blood gas level. The level of oxygen in your blood became the benchmark for getting your ticket home with us.

Over the months, the nurses, led by your neonatologist, the ever-gracious Dr. Sidebottom, cared for you. You got better and you got bigger. The first big event on your way home was the day you went off of the ventilator. The sensors said your "O2" was high, and you were breathing well, which meant you could breathe on your own---and that you did when they finally removed the tube from your throat. We could then hear you cry for the first time, and that was astounding to us. At first, your little voice was very weak because your throat was sore. You cried out with a dry rasp, something like a soft but high-pitched scream. Maybe you were as surprised to hear your voice as we were. But that changed, and soon you got louder and sounded like you should. Being off the ventilator, you also got a new crib in the part of the NICU I started to call "The Feedlot." Once there, you were definitely going home, it was just a matter of time. You just had to put on some weight, and you gradually did.

But a lot of the preemies never went home. We saw many who died. Sometimes, a baby's sensor alarms would go off, and the nurses would hurry us out. There was enough distress with the parents of the preemie in trouble; they didn't want other parents seeing what was going on. After such events, we returned to your side and would see an empty crib and know that a baby had died. The absence of its parents too made us sad. Such events shook us up and made us happier you were still there.

Indeed, you were still there and were getting better each day. After a while, Dr. Sidebottom prepared us to take you home. You were active, alert, and getting bigger; big to us that is, because you only weighed 5.6 pounds. All things in life are relative.

The day you left Harris was a momentous occasion. They took that little picture of you in the blue gown. You were looking off to one direction with your hands up by your sides. There was no hair on your cute little head, but you looked good that day, and healthy. That was reward enough for the trauma of the previous three months. Even now, that picture of you is forever framed and permanently forged in my mind. Seeing you now, one would never know what happened after your birth. It proves time does literally heal, miracles are possible and life does go on, no matter what.

It does go on and not just for you. Your neonatologist, Dr. Sidebottom, is still at Harris. I saw him on the TV news one day, and he looked almost the same. His hair was grey, but he had the same gentle eyes, smile, and soft voice that comforted your mom and me so many times. His skills and kind ways are the main reason you are here today and will have a normal, happy and long life.

One day, you too will have grey hair like him. And when that day comes, remember what he and the other doctors and nurses did for you. Be glad of that, and do your best to selflessly help someone around you, just as he and the others at Harris did for you and us, so long ago.

Roger Barfs in the Car

To Roger:

One summer day, we went over to Grandmama's to spend the afternoon. It was a hot day; and after some time in the pool, we decided to head back home.

I do not remember if you felt bad over there, after going there so many times, but on the way home you became ill. You were in the back in the car seat and we could see you were not feeling very good.

When we were driving, on the now demolished I-30 overhead on the south end of downtown, you threw up. You erupted, and a huge, long stream of white vomit went all over you, the car seat, and the upholstery of the old blue Buick's backseat. You gurgled and cried out in anguished baby talk. I drove faster.

One of the most vivid memories was seeing you in my rear-view mirror. You were still strapped in the car seat but had a look of abject agony on your face, a pathetic visage of hurt, dismay and discomfort. You had some kind of cereal earlier, and the half-digested chunks of it covered your blue Oshkosh overalls. A horrid stench of sour stomach juices wafted through the car. It was not a very pretty sight or a very pleasant smell.

Luckily, we got home quickly and got you out of the car and inside. After you were bathed and settled down, I went back out to the driveway to clean up the Buick, which was certainly a mess.

I took the car seat out of the car and placed it on the driveway and turned on the garden hose and sprayed off the mess. I cleaned the car upholstery off. After some time and effort, the car seat and car were returned to normal. And you felt better, too.

That was not the last time you were sick in your life, but that time sticks in my mind to this day since it was unique. Your past stomach problem caused me a case of indigestion that lingers to this day—it is an ill with no cure. And honestly, I do not want any relief from it. Forgetting that day would deprive me of something that we both now laugh about. So whatever made you frown in agony that day still puts a smile on our faces now. Yes, even vomit can be nostalgia.

Jeffery W. Turner

Sebastian the Crab

To Jane:

You always loved animals of all types—from big ones to little ones, from dogs to cats, and even crabs; Hermit crabs, that is. Specifically, one in particular you called Sebastian.

How you got Sebastian is a story. When I was dating Denanne, you kids went with us on a short vacation to see her parents at Port Aransas near Corpus Christi. We went to Padre Island and swam and played on the beach. Roger had a seizure, as you recall, and scared us all to death, prompting your mom to fly down to be by his side. On a happier note, we ate freshly caught blue crabs and other tasty seafood. And other good food at that small BBQ joint on the way there—the famous Luling City Market. All in all, a very good time.

One afternoon, we toured the small nautical museum in Port Aransas. That was for me, being a museum fan, not so much for you kids. We walked around inside and looked at the exhibits, which was fun for me, but probably boring for you and Roger. However, that did not last, at least for you. That change in outlook came from the gift shop. Besides books on ships and other seafaring knick-knacks, they sold live hermit crabs and the related items to feed and care for them.

Seeing the little creature and prompted by the lady who worked in the gift shop, you were instantly enthralled by the creatures and begged me to buy you one. I feared it would die after purchase, but the ever-informative lady chimed in to counter that. Hence, I decided to buy you one, its habitat, and the related food and care items.

We loaded the crab and its stuff in the car and left. I think you had the stuff in your lap or by your side. That physical closeness to the crab showed what was to come. You really cared for the crab and truly enjoyed it. You quickly named it Sebastian after the crab in *The Little Mermaid* Disney flick–which you loved.

We returned home from the coast, and you took Sebastian home to The Colony and set him up in your room. He was in a little aquarium with gravel and a little castle-like thing in it. With his food nearby, his new home was now carefully set up for his safe existence far from the predators of the sea. And exist he did—for a lot longer than I thought he would; about a year.

Each time I came over to The Colony to pick you up, you mentioned him. Many times you took me to your room to see how he was doing. You would pick him up, gently pet him, and explain how crabs actually liked that. Apparently so, he never appeared to be in stress when he poked his nose out of his shell. I think you even brought him to my house a few times and showed me how he liked being petted even more. You really loved that little crustacean, and you cared for him daily and dearly.

Even so, Sebastian met his end. Not from a lack of care or being devoured, but most likely from a disease that came from the other crab you bought to be his roommate. Pearl was its name. Soon after Pearl moved into "Crabville," Sebastian died. You were very sad and missed him. Pearl did not last long either. You were *crabless* then, and "Crabville" forever remained empty—you never had another crab.

As I mentioned, you always loved animals, all animals as far as I knew. That love for the fauna around us is still with you today. Not just for animals that are pets—like your beloved dogs Jewel and Tonk—but for animals you will deal with in school and in your future.

Majoring in marine biology is an outward sign of that inward passion. Maybe I should have foreseen you pursuing such a career then. In retrospect, Sebastian's time was just an early hint of what would become your dream. Your care for a little crab showed how you would be interested in such animals as an adult. Regardless of how such things may have led to your chosen profession, how that little crab made you happy. Here's to hoping that the crabs and fish you work with after college will make you smile as big, and as much, as Sebastian.

Dad's Diabetes

To Roger and Jane:

You two have always known I had diabetes, a disease that I have had for 27 years. While one of my doctors is surprised I am still here, I have not had too many issues with it since I tend to eat right and exercise. It is something I have adapted to in many ways. But the most important thing I do, which keeps me sane and not down about having a disease that is ultimately fatal, is poking fun at it. Yes, making light of a thing that may kill me. It is "gallows humor", if you will, and something I did around you when you were little. Here is one example of that dark art.

When you were very young, you saw me take my insulin shots. Being kids, and not knowing what it really was, you were curious. In the mornings especially, you would see me sit down and stick one of my syringes into my leg. Since you had shots at Dr. Scroggie's, which hurt, you wondered how I could do that without flinching. It really did not hurt much unless I did it wrong, but more than once I threw the syringe into my leg like a dart with your eyes wide open in silent horror and amazement.

I would shoot the insulin in, pull the medical dart out of my leg, and wipe off any small amount of blood that might appear. You were silent and amazed, but I explained that it didn't hurt, and I had to do that to stay alive and healthy. You seemed to accept that and honestly neither of you ever mentioned my disease much at all.

By that silence, perhaps, I made my ultimate point. That is, that when something bad happens, you should try to make light of it if you can. In finding humor amongst the dark shadows of hardship, you can find a light that shines a path away from hardship and despair to safety and peace. Throwing that syringe into my leg in front of your little eyes opened a big door to another room in my life, one that let me deal with having such a thing and more importantly appreciate some of the hardships in your lives; letting you know that, in the end, all would be okay. It always is.

Jeffery W. Turner

Strolling with Roger and Jane

To Roger and Jane:

Being diabetic, I usually went walking at night and strolled down the streets around our house, going to and fro most every day. After you were born, I still did that, but I had you with me in the blue stroller, which was a gift from one set of grandparents.

I would tell your mom goodbye and would pick one of you up and put you in, and off we would go down Monterrey Drive to somewhere around our old, beloved neighborhood.

We would usually head east and go up the hill, past the house of the famous weatherman, Harold Taft and then fork right or left to go deeper into the sea of houses there. Sometimes we would go down Morrison, the road to the New Park, and around on another street back to Monterrey.

While we went down the streets, we would talk to each other, after you were old enough to do so that is. Regardless of your ability to speak, I used those times to broaden your vocabularies. As we would see things, I would tell you what they were. Each time I gazed on something, I told you the word for it. It could be a type of flower, a type of bird, a cloud, or the name of a one of our neighbors like Jess, Madge, Jim, Anita, or Al. Both of you got into that habit, and sometimes would point at something and then look up at me wanting me to tell you what it was. Over time doing that and reading to you most every night, both of you knew more words than most kids your age.

Each of you had favorite words, too. One of Jane's was "Chinook," the name of a military helicopter (a CH-47) we saw flying over our heads. Jane called every helicopter a Chinook for a long time, by the way. One of Roger's was Mary Jane, your long-time cat. Mary Jane was originally corrupted into something like "mu-juh," but you said it just the same.

Occasionally something really funny and memorable happened while we were out. Once, I had a funny t-shirt with a Soviet red hammer and sickle with the words "Radio Moscow: Take Your Radiation Like a Man" written on it. It was an obvious reference to the Chernobyl nuclear disaster. One warm Sunday morning, I had Roger in the stroller and went by the Baptist church at the end of Morrison. Some old couple in a Cadillac turned into the church and stared. I assumed they saw the red hammer and sickle on my shirt—I had my black "Devo" style slit sunglasses on. Hence, I was clearly a "Commie-traitor-hippie", or something, in their eyes. Little did they know I was and am quite the conservative patriot, as they probably were too. They had no idea the irony of my clothing. Humor and subtext was all around, not just in the sites you were seeing.

The strolling was something simple, yet important for me and both of you. Walking is something we all do, as is talking. Both are mostly taken for granted. But the combination of strolling and teaching you new words was a larger thing and of bigger importance—an act of learning, which I think helped you both to make better grades in school. It also helped me by keeping my blood sugar under control.

Those many evenings strolling in east Fort Worth were good for us in more than one way. They gave us so many peaceful good memories. So as you walk down the streets in your own lives, look back on those times with me and the stroller. When you recall those times, one day hence, do the same with your children. Tell them these old stories and teach them new things, new words, new sights, new sounds, new smells. Perhaps they will hear that I did the same thing with you "way back in the 20th century." That way, the story of our family will keep walking down the temporal streets of eternity with those we love and will not be lost or forgotten, in the back roads of time.

Jeffery W. Turner

Mom and Dad Get Food Poisoning

To Roger:

One Saturday when you were little, your mom and I ate Chinese food for lunch at a place where we had dined many times, as did MeeMaw and Granddad Tom. That day, the pork tasted good, but didn't turn out to be.

After dinner, we started feeling nauseous and started to throw up. So much so that we knew we had food poisoning. We were to the point of being incapacitated. We called Grandmama and Granddad Harry for help.

Your grandparents arrived, and we were ready to go to the hospital. Granddad Harry stayed with you at the house while Grandmama drove us to Harris Hospital. We both had solutions in case we threw up in her car. I had an empty paint bucket, which I hugged tightly as I puked as we sped down I-30 to the emergency room (which we had been to before with you when you had bronchiolitis for a week when you were a year old).

And not too soon, we arrived at the hospital and were taken inside where a doctor examined us. Yes, we had severe food poisoning and were placed in waiting rooms, after being given shots of relief—Demerol injected with the largest and most painful needles ever invented by mankind. The medicine felt cold going in my rear, but soon my stomach was much better.

For some reason, the hospital placed both your mom and me in the same room. I can remember the surprise of one young nurse, who came in to check on us when she saw a man and a woman in the same room. How often does that happen in a hospital? The nurse was certainly shocked until I explained why. We were married, and both had bad pork at our favorite Chinese restaurant (which we never went back to, by the way. No surprise, right?) We certainly were not in the room to engage in some medical ward "hanky-panky", like I remember seeing on some TV movie when I was a kid. Then the nurse smiled a little, understood, and checked our vital signs. Still, this was not something that happened very often, and the nurses joked with us about that.

Soon enough, we got better and I went home first; your mom had to stay one more night than I did, as she had it worse. When we were back home, we grabbed our stomachs remembering the agony of the pork that made us so sick, but we also grabbed our stomachs laughing about being in the same hospital room together those nights. Indeed, the Chinese food was very bad, and we wanted to forget its dire effects. But the "yin and yang", (I know, that was bad) of the whole event was something to always remember and grin about.

Roger Never Sleeps

To Roger:

After your less than typical birth, your days as a baby at home were not very ordinary either. Most babies wake up a lot, needing a bottle or a diaper change. But after a while, they will sleep most of the night—a certain relief to the very tired parents. But you woke up a ***bit*** longer than most babies do. You did not sleep all night for an ***entire*** year after you were born. Your mom and I were simply exhausted by then and when you finally snoozed eight hours, it was a blessed event.

There were several reasons. One was that you simply did not sleep well, maybe from being sick more often, and also from the condition of your lungs which were still stressed.

But the biggest reason was the heart and lung monitor you had to wear over your little pajamas. That device was supposed to set off alarms if you stopped breathing or your heart stopped (or if it **thought** that happened). That infernal machine was a bit sensitive; it would go off if you just turned on your side or stretched out. There were many, many nights that it suddenly went off because of that. Your mom and I would awake in panic and fear and pick you up to see if you were okay. One of us would be readying the oxygen tank by your bed or thinking of doing infant CPR. In the dark at those frightening moments, nothing else mattered; we had to see how you were. Without a doubt, these alarms woke us up better than any normal alarm clock ever did.

Maybe one time you really did briefly stop breathing due to sleep apnea, as opposed to something worse. But the device going off was a regular thing and after a point, your mom and I were simply worn out. Sometimes, your grandparents would keep you one night to give us some needed rest—a night without the alarm going off. We would sleep soundly; but when we awoke, the first thing we did was call to see how *you* were. And hear about the alarm going off from MeeMaw or Grandmama. That cycle went on for months until you finally *did* sleep all night. That dreaded monitor and its alarm went from our house for good: to torment and alert some other family with a sick child by their side.

But I had to remember one thing about the monitor. While not getting sleep was bad, the thought of not having you around was far horrifying. That commonplace medical device was always a reminder that things could have been much, much worse. So when I think back, I can smile and see you as the grown man you are now, sleeping soundly all night. Most of the time anyway.

Jeffery W. Turner

MeeMaw and Granddad Tom

To Roger and Jane:

My parents, like most grandparents, were simply absorbed by you two children—absorbed in a good way since they loved you so much. Still do in the case of MeeMaw, who is still with us. My mom and dad, always the good parents to me and your aunt, were the proverbial, stereotypical grandparents who loved you very much and spoiled you rotten.

Their love and attention for you started in the tough time when Roger was born, but their un-selfish giving of their emotions and time to you extended far beyond that time of crisis and need. It went into your day-to-day lives in many ways, too.

Among other things, they loved having you in their pool in Gainesville, keeping you for the weekend, attending your school functions, coming to see you at our house, and bringing you toys and treats. Don't forget MeeMaw's muffins, something she still does from time to time.

Their love for you was not oriented just to things that were material. They would talk to you about things in your lives, both good and bad, and took an interest in you that went well beyond what a "typical" grandparent might do. They loved you both as much as they loved me and my sister, as they did your cousins.

You could sum that up by the picture that used to hang at your aunt's house in Granbury, the picture of Granddad Tom surrounded by you and your cousins in the pool in Gainesville. The gentle and happy smile on his face with all of you in his big arms shows perfectly how he **and** MeeMaw cared. Indeed, you were lucky to have grandparents like them. In this age of self-centered materialism and the "me generation," such focused love of others is not as common as it was when families lived close to each other. There was less material "stuff" people chased. Instead of *things,* my parents sought *family,* the people they loved. All of us are the beneficiaries of that great and selfless affection. For such love, we should always be thankful and try to provide the same for those important in our lives.

Grandmama and Granddad Harry

To Roger and Jane:

You mom's parents had a different style than mine had as grandparents. Not a bad departure, but their lives were different from my parents' lives. Their personalities were not the same either. Regardless of that, they loved you kids as much as my parents loved you.

Now when Roger was born, they were at the hospital as much as everyone else and just as upset. When Roger was not doing well, Granddad Harry talked to a priest about giving him last rites. The situation was that bad. That request upset me since I wanted you to be okay. But I never said anything. That aside, it showed a side of him that was a big part of his being: his Catholic faith. The Catholic Church was always deep inside him, and he felt it was important to follow its traditions. The Church was strong in his family in more than one way. For example, one of his brothers was a priest, your mom's uncle, "Brother Carl." Regardless of how religious he actually was, it was at the core of who he was as a man.

Another side of him was enjoying simple pleasures in life like his spaghetti (which I detail later in the book), his smokes, watching the LSU Tigers on TV, and despising the Dallas Cowboys with great joy. Since I am not a big sports fan, he got me interested in disliking the Cowboys, too, I might add. But LSU football was his favorite. I can still recall him shouting, "Go Tigers," with a big grin on his face and a smoke in his hand while watching a game on Saturday. He certainly loved all sports, but football was his favorite.

Now your grandmama liked the finer things in life more than Granddad Harry. She enjoyed having nice clothes and liked shopping over at Ridgmar Mall or Hulen Mall near where they lived. She bought you clothes and toys as well. On some of her drives to places, she would get lost and call your mom or me to get directions. That was something that drove your mom nuts. Grandmama was also more outgoing and social than Granddad Harry. Granddad Harry was content to be quiet and watch TV, but Grandmama liked to go to happy hour or attend a party; your mom got that from her, I guess. Now your grandmama is still alive as I write this, and she still takes an interest in you both—sometimes not in a way that you like when she lectures you about the right type of profession. But, be assured, she wants only good things for you and loves you dearly.

On holidays, we always had a "tree" with them like we did with my parents. There would be a turkey, some ham, and the ever-present green bean casserole at the table. We would sit down and eat and open presents. Like most grandparents, there would be a ton of toys for you around the tree. Your grandparents loved you very much, and Christmas was one time when that great affection was seen.

Your grandparents were not always available to keep you since they had regular jobs unlike my parents. When they did keep you, it was usually on a Saturday night, and your mom and I would go out to dinner or a date. Sometimes, we went to their apartment and had Sunday lunch and swam in the pool. Pastoral and pleasant times were had on those hot summer days.

Now I have been writing this like you were around Granddad Harry as much as Roger was, Jane. But sadly he never saw you since he died the Christmas before you were born. I wish that had not happened because he was most eager to see if you were a boy or a girl. After Roger's tough time, everyone hoped your birth would be routine. Granddad Harry was just as interested as the other grandparents to see you come into this world without harm. In short, he adored you (and Roger, of course) greatly even though he never had the chance to see your precious little face. I really wish you had been able to be around him. Writing about these things like you were there might help you picture what others have told you about him. Hopefully if there is an afterlife, you will then have a chance to ask him yourself about these stories and see how much he loved you both.

In the end, your mom's parents loved both of you and always had a deep amount of care for you. Yes, they were different people than my parents, but you know the saying, "Vive la difference." Indeed so, you should celebrate who they were and be glad they were in your lives.

Jeffery W. Turner

Xmas Audiology with Roger

To Roger:

When you were little, we took you to physical and occupational therapy because of your early birth, in order to catch up your development. You also saw an eye doctor and other specialists, too; plus, you had eye surgery and wore a patch over your eye to strengthen its muscles. But the one treatment I maybe remember the most was the treatment for your hearing.

Based on a variety of things, we were sent to an audiologist by Dr. Scroggie, who was your doctor. A new and different type of treatment was recommended to improve your hearing. Plus, it was not a one-time procedure, like a surgery or a weekly trip like your OT and PT. Instead, you had to go to an office twice a day for a week to get a one-hour treatment using sound. The treatment played back sound with varying tones to make your ears respond, exercising them in a way, which would improve your hearing and cognition. Your mom and I discussed this technique and agreed to have it done.

Since your mom and I both worked, we decided to do the treatments over Christmas. I had some spare vacation days, so we decided I would take you over to Addison twice a day for the period prescribed. So it began, one weekday after Christmas.

We would get up, your mom would head out the door to work, and you and I would pile in my car and drive over to Addison off of Beltline Road, near where I then worked. We would arrive around 9 or 10AM, after rush hour. In we would go. Since I could not be in the room with you, I would go back to the car and read or listen to the radio. When you were done, we would drive home, have some lunch, and turnaround and go back there again. In the afternoon, I would do the same thing: take you in, go back out and read, get you after it was over, and drive back home before the tidal wave of cars flooded the roads during rush hour. So it went for many days.

It was a less than relaxing Christmas break since commuting twice a day was not much fun. But that was okay; merely having you around was the biggest present one could have. If you had not been there, Christmas would have not been the joyous time it is now when we are together and can loudly and clearly hear each other's words. Your "new ears," as your mom called them, seemed to work just fine. That was a precious enough gift for me.

MeeMaw's Cooking

To Roger and Jane:

Something that has been a huge part of all of our lives is MeeMaw's cooking. My mom, your paternal grandmother, is a very good cook who cooked not just for the pleasure of it, but because she simply loved us. In one simple act of baking a cake or making something new for dinner, she reflected and offered her love. She still does.

Cooking, because she cared for us was not just done at holidays or birthdays. She cooked on typical and ordinary days, too. One of the best examples was the muffins she has made for us. Even now with you grown, she will bake some goodies and get them to you. She makes them for me, too, and did that before you were here in this world.

As far as holiday fare went, who can forget the "MeeMaw Dip"? Secret finally revealed, it's actually a recipe created by my third grade teacher Mrs.

Norma Cole, whose husband Buddy worked with Granddad Tom. But we all credit MeeMaw with its creation every holiday when it is there for the assembled clan to consume. It never lasts long. And as for her other treats, like the baklava? Well, that one started when I was a kid and continues to this day. Usually, she cooks that just at Christmas, but that was not always so. We all do love it.

Besides holiday grub, she always cooked your favorites on your birthdays or other times, too. There were the fried chicken fingers, canned corn, homemade mashed potatoes, and fresh cream gravy for Jane. For Roger, there was a favorite that was mine as well, which was the "Billie Sue Chocolate Cake." That cake was an old fashioned chocolate cake. The icing was actually cooked. Billie Sue McLaughlin was a relative of MeeMaw's who we knew long ago.

As far as non-holiday or special occasion fare goes, or for any menu that is, when did you ever have something bad to eat cooked by her? I would say never; even when she thought something was bad, it was usually not bad. At worst, her cooking on a bad day was above average. At best, well, you know.

Also, she has always been willing to try something new in the kitchen. On more than one occasion, she has conjured up something she has never done before and presented it to us to consume. The dishes were usually nothing fancy or gourmet, but they were original and tasty nonetheless. There was always something new to try; even though like most of us, she has her personal favorites like fish, especially salmon and catfish, and red wine—a good cabernet sauvignon, of course. Let's not forget a cold gin and tonic, speaking of drinks. I digress.

You can now see MeeMaw cooked all of her life. It made an impression on me and your aunt; why do think we all can cook so well? We have all partaken of her cooking skills one way or the other, and our bellies and souls are both full because of the fine taste. Many eat well, but have no love in their life; but we have both, because of the love shown by the cooking she so loved to share.

So when you say grace over a meal years from now, include her in your thanks and remember her every time you have a fine meal with your families. Better yet, do some cooking for the ones you love, just as she did for you.

Granddad Harry's Spaghetti

To Roger:

Your MeeMaw and Granddad Tom cooked a lot, and Grandmama cooked some too; but your Granddad Harry cooked one thing alone— spaghetti, just that and nothing more. While that was his sole culinary feat, it was something to behold.

It was a special dish. Not for having a huge set of exotic ingredients, but simply because he loved it so, and it was simple to make. It was his favorite meal. He liked it more than his old US Army favorite, the much and wrongly maligned "shit on a shingle." It was his love of that meal that made it good.

Most Saturday nights he cooked it. We would go to your grandparents for dinner and see him by the stove stirring away. He first browned the meat, adding some spices. Nothing fancy mind you—just some salt, pepper, garlic, or maybe some Lowry's, but that was all.

After that, onions would go into the mix, and then the canned tomatoes. Nothing more would go into the pot, it just simmered away. That was it, simple as simple could be—a meat sauce with maybe six or seven ingredients.

But it was more than just those few things in the pot. It blended into something much, much more. Those few things turned into something that was simple in construction but complex in result: A tasty and filling unity of victuals in our bowls.

In the bowl it went over the noodles. A slice of French bread was by its side. We would sit down together and scoop it up and be filled up quite well.

There was desert, too. What I remember more than ice cream or cake was your granddad having a smoke in his chair with the TV on after a meal. His belly was full of the sauce he made and he was content as could be, as he pulled a drag on his cig with his dark framed glasses on. With a cold Miller Light on hand, he sat content on his throne, and seemed well with the world for a time.

They say simple things are best in life. That is true. A simple bowl of spaghetti cooked by someone that loved you embodies this important truth. Such things are remembered better than an expensive gift like a ring sometimes. Now that sauce lives on in the same way–a small, yet simple thing, that lives large with me still. So when you make spaghetti one day hence, remember Granddad Harry well. I think he would approve.

Jeffery W. Turner

Granddad Tom's Smoker

To Roger and Jane:

As you know, I like to smoke meat on my little Brinkman smoker in my back yard. While it is not large or fancy, the Brinkman does the trick because it can easily handle both a turkey and a ham at the same time. A lot of people spend hundreds or even thousands of dollars on smokers and grills; but at $80 to $100 each, the Brinkman is a good value. Using a smoker is not something I saw on TV and thought, *Hey, I gotta get one of those.* Instead, it's something I started doing because my dad used one. Granddad Tom loved using smokers, so do I.

When I was a kid when we lived in Ranch Estates at MeeMaw and Granddad's first house, there was a large, brick grill by the patio. I remember Granddad cooking burgers and his always beloved steaks on it while drinking a cold Schlitz beer. After a few years, it was torn down for some reason—we'll have to ask

MeeMaw about that. A smoker arrived on the scene to replace it—a "Mr. Smoker" brand to be exact. Granddad had that thing for many years and used it frequently for smoking things like turkeys and hams and grilling the ever- present steaks he enjoyed so much. Being from a poor family, steak was a luxury to him, and we seemed to have steak once a week.

Mr. Smoker came with a short instruction booklet, which explained how to smoke many types of things. I have the now worn pamphlet and *still* use it to see how to cook types of meat—an antique that I still have in my recipe file by the white microwave. You can tell its age by looking at the man on its front cover wearing 1960's "golf schlock" attire.

One thing to remember, in the 1960s, smoking meat was not as widespread. Why? I am not sure; but it sure caught on, and most members of our family still do it. It has become an unspoken tradition for us and smoked turkeys and hams have adorned most every Thanksgiving and Christmas for decades. Many memories were created around the curves of the smokers that have been part of our households. While not cherished, they are still almost loved because they really were where most of our holiday family meal fare came from.

The act of using a smoker was part of the holiday activities. When I was older, I remember many dark, cold nights, standing by the smoker with my dad. The smoke would wrap around us if the wind blew right, while we sipped some Jack Daniels and water and talked about just about anything, including you kids and your cousins.

To me, that, is the real story about Granddad's smokers. The food was always good, well, *usually* good since there were some disasters (like when the fire went out). But the memories of standing there with your granddad are what now taste the best, in a sense. The memories of him, the smokers, and their tasty fare are what loom large. It teaches us all that doing something simply, slowly and quietly with your kids and family can be much larger than it appears. Hence, remember that in the years to come with your own families, and light a fire around a smoker to see what pleasing things come out of it that you and yours will always treasure. May your turkeys and hams always turn out like you hope, taste as good as you desire, and fill your family with love.

Jeffery W. Turner

Your Rooms at My House

To Roger and Jane:

After me and your mom split up, I had my own places. Whether it was an apartment or a house, I always had bedrooms set up for you. When you visited me, I wanted you to have your own space and your own things. Hopefully that would help those times with me seem more like you were still at home.

Over the years, your rooms at my homes had the usual stuff: a bed, a closet, and some other furniture like a little desk. Honestly, I did not spend a lot on those furnishings, but they seemed to work fine. You both had toys in the closet and a place to sit to do your homework. And you had your own TVs and later on stereos too. There were pictures on the walls as well. Yes, most were ones I already had, but each of you had one I had in my own room growing up – the sand dollar in Jane's and the B-29s in Roger's. When we weren't doing something together, you two would sit in your rooms, play with your stuff, and talk on the phone to your friends or your mom. All in all, you had normal surroundings at my home where things were usually calm.

When you went home, you would straighten up your rooms, pack up your stuff, and off we would go back to Plano or The Colony to take you back to your mom and away from your home away from home—your home with me. As kids, you had two homes, you see.

While I had the rest of my houses to myself, your rooms were still yours, even if you were not in them much, especially when you were in college and grown. Your rooms are still there now. They are filled with your remaining stuff—Jane has more in hers—but those bedrooms remain yours not mine, even though they are surrounded by the rest of the house, which I alone now silently tread.

Even though I am the only one here, your doors are open, and your things remain. The rooms are still and quiet now, but in my mind, I still can see and hear you in them. When I walk into them, I can remember you sleeping in your beds, watching TV, reading a book, or eating a snack. The chalk portraits of you by your bathroom door are another reminder of those times. Those thoughts and images are echoes of your childhood that fill your rooms and my mind every single day.

So what now for your rooms you ask? Being single and with you two grown, there is no day- to-day need for them to remain as is. But they will remain yours as long as I am there. Maybe in not too many years hence, you might be back in them more—not by yourselves, but with a yet unknown spouse and maybe some kids of your own. When that day comes, your rooms and my house that were once filled with the sounds of your little voices and youthful games, will see that again. That is how your bedrooms at ***my*** house, which is also ***yours***, should always be.

Notes To My Kids: Little Stories About Grown Up Kids

Bricks with Names

To Roger and Jane:

When you were young, the Fort Worth Public Library was engaged in a project to revamp and expand the downtown Central branch. It was in the early 1990s, and they were short of money to do this ambitious project. As a result, they began a rather unique fundraising effort. This was the sale of bricks, with people's names or wishes inscribed on them, which would be placed on the building's sidewalks. Since I was a regular patron of the branch, I decided to buy one for each of you. Thus the "Bricks with Your Names" were born.

I remember going downtown to the branch and writing out the check and filling in the forms with what I wanted the bricks to say. As you know, I put your full names on them. Some months later, the bricks started appearing around the edges of the building; and one day, I went there, and I saw yours in the area they call "Peter Rabbit Court" on the south side of the building on 3rd Street. Your bricks were not next to each other but were just a few feet apart. More than once I took you to see them. But like most little kids, you were not particularly excited about them; you were more focused on things like getting me to take you to McDonalds or Charlie's Pizza for lunch. I bet I was not the only parent who was greeted with such a lack of appreciation!

Many citizens bought these bricks and are now around the perimeter of the redone and stately façade of the building, which unfortunately had several bad water leaks and took even more time and money to repair. You could walk over the bricks and see the names of other people, both young and old, and I wondered who they were. What kind of people were they? What memories were enshrined by these little monuments under my feet? These little bricks were the signs of other lives and the host of memories that went with them.

When I see your bricks even after so long—I still visit them—they make me go back through the years and think of you when you were little. In their innate smallness, they now paint the large canvass of your early lives in my mind. These little bricks will make those times live on in a way, perhaps when you visit them one day with your own yet-to-be-born kids. Also maybe in the minds of others who never knew us as they too walk over them in silence as I have done many times. Maybe they will wonder who the other people were, the people with their names on the bricks at the library downtown.

Jeffery W. Turner

Jane Walks Early

To Jane:

In many ways, you were the total opposite of Roger. Roger was born premature, had a difficult time, and it took him longer than usual to learn to do things. You, on the other hand, did things earlier than was typical for an infant or toddler of your age. One of those things was learning to walk.

You learned to crawl early; you would crawl and scoot around the house when you were but a few months old. Like most babies, once you learned to crawl, you started to grab hold of the side of the furniture and try to stand up and walk like your brother and Mom and Dad.

One night when MeeMaw and Granddad Tom were over at the Monterrey house, you took your first real steps, albeit with a little help from the rest of us. You were maybe six or eight months old, which was very young to be trying to walk. But you did. We sat on the floor of the den with you held by one of us. Then we would turn and set you free toward one of us. You walked on your own in the desired direction and one of us grabbed you before you would tumble. Each time you waddled across the carpet we would smile, shout, and clap at your rather astonishing feat. You could sense what you were doing and had a giant smile on your little face, as you took each step and made joyous goo-goo-gah-gah noises. You were walking, even with some help from us, and it was a very big deal.

Even though there is an old VHS tape someplace with that eventful night recorded on it, it is one memory that I can replay in my head without a tape to remind me of the scene. The image is still clear—funny how small steps make for huge memories.

Roger Goes Potty

To Roger:

Every little kid is trained to go to the bathroom on their own. Until then Mom and Dad have to lend a hand. Literally, as you know, by sitting you up on a toilet or performing the more personal acts of cleaning diapers and getting your little behind clean with a handful of wipes. Now I won't go into the many jokes and gross things I said to your mom about you and your sister's baby poop being guacamole or chili but let us remember the day you went to the potty all by yourself, producing a "number two."

Your mom and I had bought you a training potty and set it up in our bathroom downstairs. The little, white potty sat next to the larger adult "throne" on the floor. We would sit on the adult "throne" by it and encourage you to relax and do your business there and not go in the diapers you still wore. Like many little ones, you were reluctant to do that. Maybe you were scared and feared the bowl would devour you or flush you to your doom, or maybe you just did not have the confidence to literally let *go* and get things done.

At some point, your mom and I got frustrated with you. We sat you down on your potty when you said you had to go—at least you had that down—but you would sit without any results. Ultimately, we would pick you up, and you went in your diaper much to our dismay.

We also resorted to bribery of sorts. We promised you we would buy the big, red, battery-powered jeep you could ride in from Toys "R" Us.

But one night, we were extra firm. You got frustrated, too; we told you that you HAD to go in the little potty, and we would not let you up until you did. This went on back and forth for some minutes, but then a miracle happened to use the old cliché. You turned red, straining and making some noise, and lo and behold, a potty was born.

You shouted out in glee that you had gone poo-poo on your own and made us come near. Grabbing some wipes to be ready, we lifted you up; and indeed, there was real stool down below. You had gone number two on your own, and we were all very pleased.

We made this a big deal with you, clapping, smiling, and saying well done. You would have thought you had squeezed out a bar of gold. But in that small and very human act, you made one of your big steps away from being a baby and towards being a much happier, little toddler. Plus that red jeep showed up and became one of your favorite toys you, and later Jane, rode around in for years after that. And that story my son, is no shit.

Watching Disney, Barney, and 'Toons

To Roger and Jane:

In the decades since the invention of TV and its now near universal presence in homes, parents and children gathered in front of the so-called "boob tube" to watch cartoons and movies. Just like my dad would watch Bugs Bunny with me on Saturday mornings, your mom and I would sit down and watch a variety of shows with you. Some of the ones I remember the most are the various Disney movies, Barney, and the Ninja Turtles.

Now, the Ninjas are easily remembered because I liked them too. I would sit with Roger while he would be enthralled by their antics, martial arts feats, and cool talk. We also watched their movies many times as well. They were as common in our house as Bugs and friends had been when I was young.

The Disney movies were something you both liked. As an adult, they drove me nuts after seeing them fifty times with you; I had seen some of them as a little kid, albeit on the big screen before the dawn of tapes in the home. Indeed, Thumper, Snow White, Lady and the Tramp, and the Dalmatians all filled our TV screen over the years. So many times, I bet I could still recite some of the scenes and dialogue even now.

In comparison to these pleasant shows, there was the **_horror_** of Barney, the purple and pink dinosaur. Truly, I despised this babbling, goody-goody lizard and all that he did. While you two were glued to the screen when he sang his famous songs, I wanted to either pass out, shoot myself, or go deaf and blind to remove myself from the video torture I was forced to endure. Indeed, I would have rather been burned at the stake than witness the idiocy that unfolded on each long and dreadful episode. I also made remarks to Mom about how I would terminate Barney, summarily execute his creators, and implied that Barney was a sexual deviant as well. I uttered not one kind word about this horrible creature. He was not a normal T-Rex, but his evil was far worse than any man-eating lizard shown in *Jurassic Park*. But now decades after I have last watched Barney with you, I can think back to when I was a kid, and I bet my mom or dad had the same feelings about some of the shows I watched with them. I would guess they did not like Johnny Quest, the Star Trek cartoon, or even Scooby Doo. But, like them, I sat through such things simply because I loved you both. Even a rotten cartoon, or one watched a million times, or a despised dinosaur does not dampen a father's love, you see. If I see something on one of those shows, I am reminded of you when you were little and how much I love you still. But I must tell you, I'll love you only as long as you don't make me watch Barney with your now unborn children. A parent's love does have its limits, when it comes to purple dinosaurs anyway.

Jeffery W. Turner

Autographed Pizza Box

To Roger:

How many kids had the proprietor of a pizza place autograph a pizza box for them? Not too many, but you did at Charlie's Pizza one day.

Charlie's Pizza was a neighborhood institution on the east side of Fort Worth. For over thirty years, Charlie and his family owned it and produced New York style pizza for us BBQ- and-Mexican-food-obsessed Texans. His pizza was always fresh and delicious, topped with fresh ingredients and a good, thin crust. It was very tasty, and we ate there frequently, as did many who lived on that side of town. In fact, one year it was voted as "best pizza" in Fort Worth.

Over time, you were old enough to realize what Charlie's was, and you specifically asked for it. You also knew who Charlie was, because we ate there many times. You would always be happy when we announced we would be eating there and ate your share of each pizza pie. Like us, it was one of your favorite places to eat and remained so over the years.

However, the most memorable thing about Charlie's was the time you wanted Charlie to autograph one of the pizza boxes. You were very insistent about this. So one day, I asked Charlie to sign one, containing a large pizza we had ordered. Charlie looked at me funny, and I explained why. He smiled real big, whipped out a pen, and ascribed his John Henry on the top of the box. I took the pie home in its box and showed it to you. You loved it and kept the box for years, sauce stains and all, in your closet. It was a valued treasure in your little boy eyes, even though it started as a plain pizza box.

Over the many years since then, the box disappeared in house moves, but the act was not forgotten. A couple of years ago before he sold his business, I was in the restaurant; and like so many times before, Charlie, now grey-headed, was behind the counter, making pies. He took my money, and I saw the stacks of empty pizza boxes behind him and asked him if he remembered signing a pizza box many years ago. He paused briefly and said with a big grin on his face that he did recall. I refreshed his memory about how happy that made you. He got a laugh about that and said no one else had ever asked him to do that as long as he had been in business.

So a plain, ordinary pizza box, just one of billions like it, was signed and treasured by you—like an autograph penned by a famous movie star or athlete. That small act of kindness by Charlie Langdon shows us that the real star on life's grand stage is not always someone well- known and famous, but instead can be an average person. Indeed, Charlie was an average person, but he was still someone very important in the big, bright eyes of a little boy named Roger, who liked pizza, and was the real star back then, and still is today.

Dr. Scroggie

To Roger and Jane:

Every little kid has a pediatrician. I remember mine, the good and kind Dr. Patterson in Denton, and you kids had one, too—namely the also good and kind Dr. William Scroggie. We started taking Roger to Scroggie since Dr. Sidebottom at Harris Methodist Hospital recommended him. Dr. Scroggie saw many children who had been born early like Roger. Later when you were born, Jane, Dr. Scroggie was your doctor, too.

As are most kids in America these days, your mom or I took you to his office for colds, shots, and sometimes something worse. Scroggie also was the first source of referrals for you; Roger had the most of these special needs.

I can remember most of these trips to see the good doctor. His nurses were kind and patient, like him. His bedside manner was calm and to the point. Your mom and I always liked and trusted him. When he was on vacation, his partners filled in for him. While these other doctors were just as competent as Bill Scroggie, he was *your* doctor, and *no others* were as special as he was. You both liked him, too; you were not afraid of him at all. Of course, you never liked hearing that you were getting a shot, but you never held that against that good man, who helped you both so much.

Over the years, you grew up and your mom moved off to Plano. So Dr. Scroggie was seen no more. I suppose he has retired by now and hopefully is well. One might think he has lots of grandkids to tend to and diagnose. I would like him to see you two now as the adults you are so he could see how well his former patients were. Perhaps in that way, you could treat *him*. A smile from two grown people who were once screaming, sick little kids might make him feel better if he was feeling the weight of the years on his shoulders or was ill. That is, a simple smile from someone is perhaps the best medicine that can be prescribed. In that sense, we can all be doctors and heal others, just like he did.

Jeffery W. Turner

Mrs. Travis at Sycamore School

To Roger:

When you were old enough for elementary school, your mom and I looked around for a place that offered programs that would help you catch up developmentally. You were smart, but your premature birth made it harder for you to learn. You needed a specialized school environment with unique teachers who could get you going. After a lot of searching, we decided on enrolling you in The Sycamore School in southwest Fort Worth, not so far from Hulen Mall and where Grandmama and Granddad Harry once lived.

Your teacher was Janette Travis, Mrs. Travis of course, who all of us came to respect and love so much. Like many teachers who taught elementary school well, she was a combination of teacher, grandmother, boss, nurse, and friend. She had structure in her lessons and knew how to connect individually with you and your classmates, like your friend Curtis.

I remember the parent-teacher conferences we had with her at the school. She was kind but still matter-of-fact in how she held them. She went over your scores and behavior with us. She pointed out the areas where you excelled and the ones where you still needed help. She gave *us* homework to do, which consisted of things to do with you to build up your skills that sometimes lagged behind your age group norms. Your grandparents also helped with these at home lessons and activities too. In short, the entire family taught you along with Mrs. Travis.

Over time, you settled into school at Sycamore. You enjoyed going there, loved Mrs. Travis, and we could see you grow. Indeed, you were a happy little boy there surrounded by a safe place and a loving teacher.

As you got older, you finally left the Sycamore School and our beloved Mrs. Travis. Even though she is a memory now, I know you still remember her. She was your first grade teacher and therefore, has a special place in your heart. I still remember my first grade teacher, Mrs. Noles, so I know you will always fondly recall Mrs. Travis. You should always treasure her dear memory because she ***truly*** helped you become the smart and talkative young man you are today. Her lessons became ***life*** lessons because they helped you in ways that still affect you now.

The New Park

To Roger and Jane:

At the old house on Monterrey, one could climb over the back fence and walk into the park on Sandy Lane if you wanted to. While we did not get to the park that way, I took you two kids there many times. That park, however, began to show its age and sometimes less than law abiding citizens went there. Thus, over time we went there less and less.

We stopped going there almost entirely when the city built a new park at the end of Morrison north of I-30 by the fire station. It was new indeed, and we started calling it, "The New Park"; the Sandy Lane Park became "The Old Park" as a result. The New Park has a name, Cobble Stone Trail Park, but we never called it that. Over the years, "The New Park" name stuck to that pleasant piece of earth not so far from the old house.

The New Park was a fun place for you each time we went there. Unlike older parks, which had just swings and a slide, this one also had wooden structures kids could climb, all nestled up against a small forest of post and blackjack oak trees that was part of the Cross Timbers that draped Fort Worth's east side.

I would push you on the swings, and you would climb over the wooden jungle gyms that were there. Jane, being more coordinated sometimes, amazed me by seeing where she would climb. Roger, you were more conventional, but you enjoyed the stuff just as much. Sometimes I would take your bicycles there. You would peddle up and down the long and curved sidewalk, going back and forth until you got tired. In fact, many of your bike riding lessons took place there.

Besides the exercise we got, sometimes we took a picnic lunch and ate it on the picnic tables underneath the big trees by the sidewalk. I took some cold beer with me on a hot day in the summer—bought at Best Mart, of course.

Since the park adjoined someone's horse farm, we petted the horses, too. We would go up to the fence, and the horses wandered over. You would reach up and pet their noses, and we fed them carrots or sugar cubes. At first, you were afraid the horses would bite you, but when you saw me do it and tried it yourselves, those fears went away. The New Park was more than just a playground because of things like that—you learned something new.

That little park was full of things to do that built many memories of how you were when you were little. But of course, you both grew up, moved away, I moved too, and we did not go there anymore. But that is not entirely true either. As I got older, I sometimes stopped by there on the way home. I would pull into the parking lot and would get out and walk around with the memories of us flooding back into the present time. I could see you running around and having fun like you were little again. Even though you were not with me, you were there in a sense. It was as if the echoes of your childhood—yes, I've used that phrase before—were still around the swings and the jungle gym. I was transported back in time and felt I was home again and not so old. But, alas…

The New Park will remain with me always. A place filled with many cherished recollections of your young and little years—memories of many good, fun, and exciting times spent together under its shady trees. It is a place that is pleasant, comforting, and filled only with good. All of the parks in our lives should forever be that way, unlike the trying playgrounds we see so often in our lives.

Notes To My Kids: Little Stories About Grown Up Kids

At the Fort Worth Zoo

To Roger and Jane:

Many parents take their kids. Let's face it, kids love animals. Why? I do not know, but they all like kittens, puppies, farm animals, and of course, the denizens of the forest, jungles, seas, and plains, they see on TV. Outside of cuddling a gaggle of kittens or puppies, going to the zoo was the pot of gold for seeing their fauna of choice since most kids now have never been around a farm. You two were no different.

Luckily, Fort Worth has a noteworthy zoo, where we took you to see such sights with hordes of your fellow kinder and their parents in tow. Every time we went to the zoo, the drill was pretty much the same. We would go west on I-30, south on University, and park as close to the front gate as we could. We would unload the stroller when one of you was too little to walk the whole way, pay, go in, and start the tour around the crowded place.

The Fort Worth Zoo is large and even then, it was being developed into a world class place. They had some old fashioned cages. But over the years, they added more open areas and exhibits. We would walk down the paths, along its course nestled close to the winding curves of the Trinity River north of TCU. Pushing you in the old blue stroller or walking while holding your little hands, we would pass by the elephants, tigers, and birds and hear them growl and squawk amidst your many questions or fanciful requests to pet them. Of course, when one of the bigger creatures had to poop, I had to make some gross remark to your mom. She would get mad and tell me to shut- up, but that was part of the fun to me as was explaining things about the animals to you when you asked. Being out there with *you*— not seeing the latest exotic snake from Zimbabwe, Ceylon, or Tricomalee —was the main exhibit for me.

After walking around the place, we always stopped in the gift shop on our way to the car. Both of you had to have some little toy or trinket to commemorate the day. Normally, your mom and I gave in and bought you something based on your pleas and out we would go with bags in our hands.

So it went when you were still in Fort Worth and little enough to want to go there. Now you two have long ago outgrown that sort of thing, and I do not remember the last time I went there. But the zoo remains as before— crowded and popular to this day. I suspect one day hence you and I may go back there once more; this time with your yet-to-be-seen kids. I bet that when that day comes, the events will be much the same. We will go in, walk past the animals, gaze at the snakes and the birds, and buy a souvenir for the day. And if I make a joke about an elephant pooping, one of you will have to slap me, just for old time's sake.

Feeding the Fish Pennies

To Roger:

One cool and cloudy Saturday when you were little, I took you to the Fort Worth Botanical Gardens and the Japanese Gardens of the park. In that area, there is a pond system with many Japanese goldfish, the so-called Coi, in its waters. You could buy fish food and feed the always hungry aquatic beasts. And that was what we did that grey day.

You found the fish interesting, but you thought they were more interesting when you fed them. You would get some pieces of the fish food I bought from the machine and threw some of it into the pond in front of you. The fish, being used to free meals, would swarm en masse to where the food landed and swirl about in a frenzy of mindless consumption until the stuff was gone.

Over and over, we repeated that act until the food was gone. You laughed in delight at the ravenous fish that seemed to swim to you on command. But then something happened. I ran out of change to buy more fish food. Then something even worse happened. I fed the fish something that was not food, in an act that was not a good example for me as your father to do in front of his son.

What did I do, you ask? I tossed the hungry fish some pennies, one at a time to see what they would do. The all-consuming fish, not being picky about what they ate, swarmed to get the pennies. They slurped up the copper rounds, not knowing the difference. You were more humored by this outlandish act than I was and giggled away. I gave you some pennies and you tried it, too. You laughed even harder than before.

But all good things must end and I ran out of pennies, thankfully for the digestive tracks of the fish. We gathered ourselves up, left the pond, walked around the park some more, and finally left for home. We laughed together in the car all the way home about our heinous acts committed against the city's fine and innocent fish. We were both guilty: like father, like son, if you will.

Years later, you remembered that Saturday with me and laughed at what we fed the fish— pennies and all. After all, we both like "off the pond" things like that. I only hope the fish enjoyed the feeding that day as much as we did. Not sure they did, but I'm sure they lived through it.

Jane at Fall Creek

To Jane:

One of the most magical times I had with you was a day we went driving around in the country near Granbury and stopped at the bridge at Fall Creek near the Brazos River. It is a pretty place in the river bottom area surrounded by hills and fields. The creek itself is clear with a flat limestone bottom you can walk on when the water is low. Trees line the creek and are all around the banks. It's a magnificent pastoral scene.

One neat place in particular, was the field by the bridge. That field reminded me of part of my granddad's farm near Valley View, Texas. It too had a creek, a field by it, and was surrounded by trees and rolling terrain that curved up some hills. When I was in the field at Fall Creek, my thoughts drifted back to the 1960s when I was little, and I remembered the many happy times there with my family playing in the creek or being around the farm.

In this case, my thoughts came back to the present and being with you, my little girl. We looked at the creek, went onto the field, and walked around it some. It was a cool, but not cold, day in late winter, and it was nice to be outside in the sun. I don't remember what we were talking about, but I had a camera with me and took some pictures of you standing in the field. One shot in particular was timeless, since it captured the spirit of who you were as a little girl. You were standing in the field, facing the road lined with trees, assuming a dramatic pose. One hand was behind your ear and another outstretched gesturing like you were on a stage. You smiled really big and had your eyes closed, all in "grand style."

That one pose tells all about your childhood. You were full of life, funny, playful, and very loving to any animal you could find. If there is one image of you that I will always remember as a little girl that would be it. The spur-of-the-moment pose that day mirrored the spontaneous nature of your personality and showed all that you were, and still are, in fact. It was one of those pictures that a parent will always remember and hold on to in their heart as the years pass by.

That picture still sits by my desk with others of you and Roger. That happy image, which captures your soul and being, will always be a reminder of your little girl years and that pretty winter day, so long ago.

Jeffery W. Turner

Watching Mr. Hawk, Mr. Roadrunner, the Buzzards, and the Donkeys

To Jane:

Most little kids love animals. You kids were no different. However, you liked them a bit more than your brother I think. You were very interested in animals of just about any type. You're like of the fauna around you extended far beyond mere kittens and puppies. Any animal you could get close to was an animal you liked to see and hopefully pet.

One day when you and your dog Tonk were over at my house, I reflected on this and remembered five prime examples of your love for animals: Mr. Hawk, Mr. Roadrunner, the buzzards, and the donkeys in Keller, and the animal shelter in Acton. The appellation "Mr." was one of those childhood words you sometimes affixed to the objects of your youthful zoological interests.

Sometimes, we went driving around the country, looking for animals like cattle and horses. But on one occasion, we were out on Bonds Ranch Road, near the place I call "The View of Forever" in my other books, to watch the many hawks that flew around out there hunting for rabbits and rats in the pastures near the ever-growing sea of houses. Mr. Hawk was more than just one hawk. We sat on top of the hill, "The View of Forever," and watched them circle on the thermals high overhead. We saw them dart over the pastures and the cattle beneath.

They never got that close to us, but one time we did get an up close view. Going back towards Business 287 and home, I drove my pickup down a dirt road through an open gate, and sitting on a fence line was a large and beautiful hawk. We stopped the truck, and the bird strangely did not move—his fixed gaze was no doubt on something in the grass we could not see. We sat transfixed, not saying a word or starting the truck, so we would not frighten our avian guest. But that moment of silence ended; the noble bird suddenly took to flight and was gone from our sight. Regardless of his brief stay, we got a clear view of his feathers, his shape, and even his eyes. Truly, it was a sight to remember.

After the stately hawk on the fence, the buzzards we also saw were the total opposite. There was a carcass of a dead cow out in that same pasture, and a huge host of black buzzards around it on the fence, circling above, or looking at it on the ground. For some reason, they were not pecking at its flesh. Maybe they had to let it *age* a bit more before they would partake. Even so, the stench of the dead cow filled the air, or maybe it was the odor of the silent, foul birds. Nonetheless, they were interesting to watch. They did not seem to be bothered by us watching them.

There was another type of fine, feathered friend we watched more than once: Mr. Roadrunner out at Granbury. We would get in the truck, sometimes your brother went too, and go up the hill overlooking Lake Granbury where there was scrub brush, cactus, and limestone rocks. There were roadrunners there. They were hard to spot, sometimes darting across the road as we slowly drove to the north. They were interesting birds, running swiftly and low to the ground. Grey-colored shapes amidst the green of the cedar and the varied white of the limestone rocks. We went up there to spot them many times, sometimes they were hidden from our view; but each time we saw them, we smiled at their sight.

Besides the birds above, one of your favorite animals was the group of donkeys that resided in a little pasture up the road in Keller by Bear Creek Park, where I used to walk. On more than one occasion, you went walking with me and we would walk past the two donkeys there. We would stop, and they would come over wanting to be fed a sugar cube or some carrots, which we had. I remember feeding them and also petting their scraggly hides on several warm and sunny days. The donkeys were a fixture of sorts by that park; they were always there it seemed. But nothing lasts forever. After some years, they were gone. I do not know if they were sold or simply grew old and died, but I missed them and the days we had seen them together having so much fun.

The last example of your love for animals was your desire to visit the little animal shelter in Acton called Friends for Animals. Most important was that you did more than visit. The people running it liked people to come in, pet the animals, and show them some attention and love. You did by holding them and petting them many times. As you did this, you wanted to adopt each and every one of them. But that was not possible; the sad side of the epidemic of adoptable pets in shelters. If those animals had someone who had loved them like you, or even a half of what you did, many of the shelters would be empty.

Seeing you now with your dogs, Tonk and Jewel, I am always reminded of when you were little, and we looked for animals to watch. Those searches were fun and stick in my mind to this day. The beauty of an animal is something to be shared and appreciated, and those memories are something to treasure, behold, and love as well as the decade's stream past those times.

Perhaps one day you will do the same with a little son or daughter of your own. The animals you see won't be Mr. Hawk, Mr. Roadrunner, the buzzards, the donkeys, or the ones in Acton; but I suspect they will be no less special to you, just as the ones we saw and the sweet memories of them, and you now.

Seeing You Each Week

To Roger and Jane:

After your mom and I divorced, we practiced "visitation" every other week and at first, on Tuesdays and Thursdays. The divorce decree allowed you to spend the night with me on those two weekday nights, plus alternating weekends. That is before your mom moved to Plano, which made the weekday nights impossible. After that I went to see you on Wednesdays, which most fathers do. Regardless of the schedule, I always stuck to it unless I was sick, or your mom and I agreed to something else. It was a pattern that went on for years and became a regular part of our lives.

The weekend routine was nothing complicated; I would leave work early and make my way over to Plano or The Colony via the route with the least traffic. Arriving at your mom's, we would load up and would return to my part of the world, via a different route with less traffic—the time of the drive determined this choice. One route was FM1187, which you still sometimes use to come to see me. I guess taking that road so many times made an impression on you, or maybe it's just easy to use.

When we arrived at my place, you would unload your bags and go to your rooms and get settled. I would start dinner while you played or talked to me about your day and week. I would cook something you both liked to eat, but not always; but it was always homemade unless we went out to eat or had something delivered like pizza or Chinese. After we ate, we would watch movies or something on TV and then to bed.

On Saturdays, we would play, watch TV, go walking, or sometimes go see members of the family. Occasionally, we went to see a movie you wanted to see or did something special, like taking you wolf calling, which I describe later. All in all, I tried to do normal, regular things to make you feel like my house was your home.

Sundays were similar to Saturdays, except I had to take you home around dinner time. We would climb in my truck, load up, and take one of the highways back eastward. I took the highway since there is no traffic on Sundays unlike Friday. We would get to your mom's, unload, I would hug and kiss you bye, and head back into the sunset towards Fort Worth. The weekend visits were always my favorites since we were together as a family for a while, and your mere presence in my residence made it a **home** again.

As I said above, you spent Tuesday and Thursday nights with me before your mom moved. I would pick you up from school and go to my place, have dinner, help you with your homework, put you to bed after your bath, and get you up the next day for school. When your mom moved, I fell back to the typical Wednesday visit routine. I drove over, picked you up from school, we ate dinner or had a picnic in the park, took you home, then drove back to Cowtown. These weekday visits were always nice for me. Seeing you always made me happy and gave me a break from work and it's always present stress. Hearing what you did in school and were doing that week kept me up on your lives and seeing you grow up.

These cycles repeated every week. It was a wonderful thing in many ways that made many memories that I cherish dearly each day. However, like all kids you grew up and came over less often after a while. While that is a sad thing for a parent, it is part of growing up and becoming an adult. At this point in time, you both have left the proverbial nest and are living your own lives as you should. The end result is I know why my mom misses me and your aunt so much. While we are grown, she still sees us as children, in an adult sense. That is a normal thing a parent does, which comes from nurturing children from birth and seeing them grow up.

You should remember this because one day *you* will see your kids fly away from your warm, safe nest and arch over the horizon of life away from your sad, fondly remembering eyes. Then you too will see how

Jeffery W. Turner

a father feels who loves his kids and treasures their sometimes infrequent visits home.

Nicknames

To Roger and Jane:

Many of us get funny nicknames when we grow up. They are short versions of our name, corruptions of our name, or simply phrases that are plays on words using all or part of our name. Or the nickname could be derived from something we did, like my nickname "Animal" while on the high school football team, which came from the animalistic grunts I made when making a hit. Your friends can give you these names, or your family can. In your case, it was the family.

Roger being the firstborn got his first. One of them was "Bossy Roggie," since even as a young child you had a determined personality that was obvious to all. What you wanted was seldom a question. Another one was "Sneaky Snake," since you snuck around with a big mischievous grin on your face, trying to hide from Granddad Tom. Once you were past the toddler times, we stopped calling you those names, except when a story from those times was recalled. Your real name stuck, and you never really had a nickname with me or the family after that.

Now Jane, your nicknames were more varied, due to your name being more adaptable to such things or perhaps due to the generally sweet personality that you have. Thus, names like "Janester," "Jane-Poo," "Janer-baner", "Poobus", or "Poobus Baby," were invented and used. Even now, I still call you, "Janester," occasionally, but not so much now since you are grown. But it was and is a term of affection.

While we do not use these funny, little names much now, except for the occasional "Janester" above, the "naming of names" was done out of love and more importantly noticing who you were when small. While these names remind me of your childhood which recedes away as the decades march on, they are verbal snapshots of the children you once were.

As I said above, parents still think of their grown children as being small. The memories of little padding feet and happy innocent smiles shine bright in the light of the present's harsh, realistic light. In that way, I am no different. You will always be "Bossie Roggie" and "Jane-Poo" to me.

Note: Since I do not use "Roger" and "Jane's" real names, I have exercised a small bit of artistic license in this Note. But since "the naming of names" is important, their nicknames were still used, although modified some.

Jeffery W. Turner

The Actress Named Jane

To Jane:

I guess being articulate runs in our family. Do you remember I won district in high school debate two years and was in speech and drama? I could always think on my feet and speak without notes. It is something I do naturally. That skill was something I used as a grownup, too, when giving training classes to clients or status presentations to angry or idiotic executives. Sometimes, to intelligent and kind "big wheels," who do exist. I digress again.

Like me, you had the proverbial "gift of gab" and used that talent on stage when you were in high school—like father, like daughter.

As does any actor or actress, you had major and minor roles. In the British styled, comedic farce, *The Murder Room*, you were one of the leads named Susan Hollister. I think that play was the one your class did the dinner theatre thing with—the food was okay too as I remember.

As far as your lesser roles went, you were the little kangaroo, Roo, in *Winnie the Pooh* and hopped about the stage with the other characters in "Poohstumes," shall we say. The floppy ears you wore were most noticeable. Perhaps the more memorable minor role was your character in *Sweeney Todd,* getting killed off ostensibly to make English-style meat pies. I've made meat pies before, but not using people as the filler.

Regardless of the role, MeeMaw, Stephanie, and I would drive over and watch the plots unfold on Colony High School's auditorium stage. We would go in, see you before the play, get our program, and have a seat. The play would be announced, and "the show would go on."

Afterwards, we would talk to you—and Roger, too—out in the hall and sometimes take pictures of you in your thespian garb. Finally, we would say our goodbyes, give you a hug, and drive back to Cowtown with the memories of the play still in our heads.

You played more than one part in all of those plays, some big and some small. You had to act out different characters and situations for the audience at hand. You did it well, I might add.

Life is like that, too. Over time, you will be a student, a young adult, a parent of young kids, and later a middle-aged parent watching your own kids act in their own life's theatre.

In that way, life, like the theatre, has many stages to act on until your final curtain call will fall. So play your parts well, so the ultimate review written by The Great Theatre Critic In The Sky will be "well done" and remembered fondly by those still acting down on Earth in life's dramatic and eternal theatre.

Granddad Tom Dies

To Roger and Jane:

When you are young, you think your parents and grandparents have always been around and will always be around. Unfortunately, that is never true. We all get old and finally die. Such is the sad nature of life. When someone who loves you dearly passes away, the event is even sadder than it usually is. That was the case with my dad, your beloved Granddad Tom.

My dad, like MeeMaw, loved you two without a doubt and without conditions. When he was around you, you could see his eyes were filled with happiness and delight. He would play with you, take you places with him like the store close to their house to get candy and snacks, and spend endless hours in the swimming pool with you with a big smile on his face.

He was the epitome of a grandfather. He was patient when you were acting up, cared for you if you were sick, and of course, showered endless gifts on you on your birthdays and Christmas. He did not give you things and then ***not*** spend time with you like some people do; he gave and was with you because that made you happy and brought glee and variety into your little worlds.

When he got sick, I knew it was not going to end well. Roger was old enough to understand what was happening, but Jane, you were not old enough to really get what was happening. When they operated on him at the hospital in Denton, the news that he had a large cancerous mass was devastating to us all. The surgeon could not get the entire tumor; and remembering how brain cancer got my granddad, the ubiquitous "TR," I knew what was in store for him.

He started chemotherapy, which lasted for some months and wore on him like it does most people who endure it. He got sick and then felt better, and went back the other way more than once. He lost weight and looked thin. Being an athlete in the past, his physical changes were most shocking because he had always been strong and healthy (except for his colitis, which he had since he was 18). After a point, he stopped the treatment because it was not going to save him, and he was tired of fighting. He even asked his oncologist if he could "speed it up." "It" being the cancer, as you might guess. After the many trials he had been through since I was in college, I guess he had decided to struggle no longer and pass on.

The thing about this whole process that still makes me cry is the last time I saw him and talked to him. He was back in the hospital in Denton and not doing well. We knew the end was not far off. Your mom and I were about to take you to Disney World for a much needed vacation. You knew your granddad was very sick, but you were still looking forward to going there.

I went to Denton to talk to him. On his hospital death bed, he made it clear that he wanted us to go ahead and take you to Disney and not cancel the trip to remain with him. He meant it, saying we might not get another chance to do such a trip. In the end, I agreed, hugged him, told him I loved him, and drove back to Fort Worth, crying my eyes out.

I talked to your mom about what he said; my eyes again full of tears, and we decided to go to Florida, even with him near death because the cancer had spread so much. We flew to Florida and had fun with you for a few days, even though my mind was far from being at ease. I would talk to MeeMaw every day and get the latest on how he was. He was not doing well and then sunk into the coma he never awoke from. We flew back home and awaited the inevitable.

Your aunt, MeeMaw, and I stayed by his side at the hospital. MeeMaw had me shave him, even though he was unconscious. She said he never went unshaven and wanted him to look clean and not so bad– certainly, she was seeing him well and fit as he always had been before. So I got a razor and some shaving cream and gently cut his whiskers and washed his face. I recalled how he helped me when I had back surgery and thought a shave was a small way to repay his acts of assistance and love he had always given me.

We knew he was about to die because his vital signs were weakening. Early in the morning one day, we watched him take his last breath. MeeMaw bent over, kissed him, said she loved him, and started to cry, as we all did that day.

We took you kids to the funeral. It was the usual Turner/Couch affair. The funeral was at the Vernie Keel Funeral Home in Gainesville, and then the burial at Valley View Cemetery, where the rest of my family also rests—your Uncle Mike included. My uncle, who was a minister, Uncle Charles, did the service. Some of the family wanted me to do the eulogy given my gift of gab, but I simply could not do that; my emotions were too strong to do it. Thankfully the service was over, and the mourning began.

One thing that I remember the most was not the funeral or his suffering, but instead, the short dream I had right after his burial. I awoke in my old bed after seeing a brown void in my personal dreamland, where his face appeared with no body. He had a big, gentle smile on his face but said nothing at all. His image lingered for a bit, and I felt like he was saying everything was okay, live your life, and do not be so sad. We can debate if dreams come from within our minds or from somewhere else, like God or a ghost, but the vision of him was stark and real enough and made me feel less down. And life did go on.

After the burial, we stayed with MeeMaw a couple of days and helped her with some things around the house and the estate-related matters. Then we returned back home. I can still picture the sad look on MeeMaw's face, as we drove away from the house. The pool was still there, but its biggest fan would never jump in it again with the ones he loved.

In the end, we will all open and pass through the gate of forever one day. When we do, let us hope we showed the ones in our family the same love he showed you and the rest of us each day. He was not perfect—no one is—but I know he was the perfect granddad for you. For that alone, you should always be thankful for his part in your lives and remember him well.

Granddad Harry Dies

To Roger and Jane:

In contrast to the long drawn out period of time leading up to Granddad Tom's death, Granddad Harry's demise was a total surprise. He passed due to a heart attack at your Aunt Sarah's house right before Christmas in 1989, not long before Jane was born.

Even though it was sudden, we knew it might happen since he was not in very good health and still smoked like a forest fire, even though he was not supposed to. You could look at him and see he was not real healthy at all.

Even so, he still enjoyed life. He liked football and sports, plus his beloved spaghetti. He loved being around Roger too. He and Grandmama did not see you as much as my parents did, son, but they loved you as much as they did. When Granddad Harry saw Roger, his eyes would light up, and he would smile with great delight. I think the mere fact you were alive was still first and foremost in his mind. That realization turned to joy when you were near. Like other grandparents, Grandmama and he piled the presents high around the Christmas tree and your birthday cakes.

With his health, he really could not do many physical things with Roger. He did not jump in the pool with you or climb up a tree, but your presence was still important to him. The impending birth of Jane was something that lit up his tree. I remember being in the car with him going to the liquor store near our house before Christmas in 1989, and we talked about your mom getting ever- bigger with Jane and hoping the toxemia would not return once more. It was bitterly cold that year; some wondered if that put his body under stress and contributed to his death. Maybe so, but knowing with certainty is impossible. But you can know without a doubt that you both were very important to him.

At Christmas itself, Granddad Harry and Grandmama were going to go to Mississippi to visit your Aunt

Sarah and her family, plus members of their extended family around Greenville and Vicksburg. We had our "tree" with them before they left. We opened presents, ate some good food, had some drinks, and your mom and I got some gifts that were intended for the "future" Jane. They left for Mississippi, and we had Christmas with my mom and dad, plus your Aunt Terri and her brood, too.

Then we got the call on Christmas Eve and learned your granddad had suddenly died at Sarah's house. No warning, he had a heart attack and died. No warning like we had with my dad. It was the proverbial bolt from the blue. Your mom and I plus Roger headed east for the funeral. Not quite what anyone wanted for Christmas, but it came nonetheless. The family had a wake, the funeral mass, and the burial in Vicksburg, where he was born. We saw your mom's aunts, uncles, and cousins, of course, which softened her blow. We had some food and drinks and tried to laugh at things, too. Finding something funny in a time of grief is what all families do. We stayed for a few days and then headed back home.

The saddest thing outside of the loss of him itself is that he never saw you, Jane. You and he never got to know each other, and that is a shame. But such things happen in life since there are no guarantees for a Norman-Rockwell-like life for any of us. Even so, he loved you and Roger so much. As I said above, you could see it in his eyes. So look at his pictures and remember the stories about him, both of you now, and know that he cared for you so. Tell your kids about him one day to honor his life. In that, you will return the great love he showed you and honor his too short life.

Jeffery W. Turner

MeeMaw and Granddad's House

To Roger and Jane:

My mom and dad bought their house in Gainesville when I was in high school. It was a spacious four bedroom home. Later they turned the two smaller bedrooms into one large one, which was your aunt's room, making it three. The patio was enclosed and turned into a playroom with a pool table for Granddad —there are stories about him being a "pool shark" at Buzzie's Pool Hall in Valley View. Finally the beloved pool was added, along with the storeroom outside, which MeeMaw called Granddad's "doghouse." By the time you two came into the world, that wonderful house had the features that made it special for us all.

Many times, MeeMaw and Granddad took you home with them for the weekend. Sometimes, all of us would go there, including on the holidays. We did a lot things there, many of which I have detailed in this work. Regardless of what we did, the house itself was the stage those events were acted out upon.

Besides the major features of the place, the exterior itself had some interesting things. One of the most memorable was the vegetable garden in the southwest side of the yard. Granddad and MeeMaw would toil endlessly in it to produce much of the food that adorned the table in warm parts of the year. They took you out to it many times to watch them pick veggies and also pull the weeds. One thing I helped Granddad do was spread chicken shit for fertilizer and till up the dirt. I never liked working in a garden; I hated it when I was a kid and hated it then, too. But you kids loved being out there because you only saw the fun side of it with your ever-loving grandparents. We all liked the veggies too.

The house itself was a Spanish-style structure with a red tile roof and a white brick veneer. That was something I never expected MeeMaw to like because she liked contemporary things so much. The house had a long driveway to the garage and a circular driveway at the front. That is where we always parked when we were there. That drive had a ring of large cactus bordering it, too. Do you remember the story of me running over one when I was in college when it was icy outside? The final touch of the outside veneer was that the house was up on a hill west of town on a one acre lot. From the front, you could see Elm creek, the park with the zoo, and parts of town. It was in town, but it did not look that way.

As far as the inside décor went, MeeMaw's love of contemporary themes was all over the house—from the abstract paintings to the sectional divan, which she still has. There were stained wood walls, and the carpet was a medium hue. Such things would be seen as outdated now, but then it was considered cool.

One thing that sticks in my mind about that beloved house was Granddad's and my bathroom. He and I shared one, and MeeMaw and your aunt had the other. That room had a light green tile and counter plus a window looking north to the Tinsley's house and yard next door. When I was grown, I would go to the bathroom and look out that window before I left. For whatever reason, that scene was something calm and relaxing to behold. It gave me a bit of comfort that only being *home* can give.

After Granddad died, MeeMaw decided to sell the house and move near your aunt and me. I remember when she sold it, and everything was out of the house. The things in it were gone, but my head was still filled with the memories of them. Even so, with the ache of losing that happy abode, I found a small bit of solace the last day we were there. We were all about to leave and head south, and I went back into all of the rooms and looked around at the emptiness and bare walls. The absence of Granddad made that void more profound. The last room I went inside was Granddad's and my bathroom. I entered it, went to the bathroom, and like so many times before, I looked out the little window to the north and felt that everything was okay. For a short time, I was far away from that moment and back in happier days when we were all there, and things were good. Coming back to the reality of the present, I turned and went out to the car to drive back to Fort Worth. I still remember how that brief moment of peace made me feel good on that sad day when we all felt loss.

We should all have such a home in our hearts to shelter us, regardless of where we reside in our lives. That house—and the Monterrey house too—are those places for me. Over time, you too will have those places and moments as life and its ever-present chaos swirls around your head. You may wish you were safe back at home, as places and people you both dearly love, fade away. So as you age, remember them well because they are part of what paved the road for the drive to your present address in the infinite neighborhood of life.

Easter Egg Hunts with The Calhouns

To Roger and Jane:

Most, if not all little kids, love the Easter Bunny tales and Easter egg hunts. Baskets filled with candy and brightly colored eggs found on a field of grass always bring smiles and happiness to the little ones around. You were no different. Easter was always something fun and exciting to you.

One thing that made that so was the big egg hunts we had with our relatives, the Calhouns, on the Turner side of the clan. Some of them farmed and had spots on their land where the pasture was mowed and some trees were around. At such pastoral places near Valley View and Gainesville, we had many hunts when you two were young. On Easter Sunday, we would drive north up I-35 from Fort Worth and gather at one of those places with the ever-growing Calhoun bunch. My Aunt Bobbie and Uncle Billy Mac had four kids who also had kids; so when assembled, we had quite a crowd. Some of those kids had kids, thus increasing the extended family's size. So many second cousins (and now third), I have trouble keeping all of their names straight—MeeMaw can however, so when needed I have to ask her who's who in Calhoun Land.

Getting back to the hunts, we gathered early in the morning at one of the pastures and made ready for the crowd. Our cars and pickups would be scattered around some of the trees. Each separate family had its brood with baskets in tow. Some of the adults would lay out the treasures, eggs and candy galore, around plants, trees, or rocks. We avoided using cactus for camouflage, of course, but it was there, too. When the goodies were concealed, you kids would be turned loose. Seeing the energy spent by all of you, one can picture images of "The Sooners" crossing into Oklahoma in search of the best land. You youngsters were the same. You sped into the area and quickly scoured it until nothing remained except the dirt and plants that were there before. The baskets were full, and the smiles were bigger still, all in about ten minutes at the most.

After that, we sometimes had a picnic lunch under the trees. Tables were set up and filled with traditional fare like fried chicken, potato salad, and tea. A typical Texan feast was had by all. That was the adult's reward, besides seeing your smiles, for hiding the eggs and sweets.

This ritual went on for a few years, and then we stopped having them or had other things to do. Families grow and change over time, which is why these things cease. The kids begat kids who begat their own kids. Thus, each nuclear family becomes its own clan, and the parade of generations marches down the long road of time by different routes. That is a natural thing to see and is nothing to fear. You will miss not being around your cousins, aunts, and uncles; but when you grow up and have kids plus nephews and nieces to boot, it's *your* turn to set up and run the Easter egg hunts and show the younger ones how it is done. By doing that, you too will find your own

Jeffery W. Turner

Easter eggs to treasure, hidden in some pasture on happy Easters yet to come.

Xmas with Me

To Roger and Jane:

Divorce makes holidays more complicated; each spouse works out some arrangement for when the kids will be over around the rules of the divorce decree. Your mom and I usually did a type of "swap" on Christmas. One year, she would have you two in the morning to open gifts from "Santa," and I had you at night for Christmas dinner and more presents. The order was reversed the next year. That simple but effective system worked pretty well for years.

Regardless if I had you for "Santa" or not, I always did a few things the same way every year. You had stockings over the fireplace that were filled with little stuff, candy, and money. You had presents from me of various types, more cash than stuff as you got older and into your teens, plus family dinners and of course, a tree. Now, my trees were never fancy at all. I would set it up and decorate it in less than a half an hour—no more work than that was done. My "Star of David" was and still is usually an empty beer can. That was something I started doing with your mom in fact, even though she did not care for that style of decoration at all. Why mess with tradition? And see the later Note that details my trees.

Another thing I never did much was decorate the inside of the house with Christmas stuff, except for a couple of trinkets on the mantle. One you still see is the set of four letters that spell "Noel" that I always turn into "Leon" as a joke. Those letters stay up all year, I never take them down. The other thing I put up is the Santa tapestry MeeMaw gave me I hang by the stockings. And of course, setting up Christmas lights is something I have willfully done maybe twice when single. I guess I am sort of a Scrooge, especially when I tell my buddies my traditional Christmas greeting of "Have a Merry Shitmas and a Crappy New Year!!" I never send out Christmas cards either. There's no reason to be jolly, you know.

Let's not forget my horrible gift wrapping skills either. Like decorating the tree, if I can't do it quickly, I won't do it at all. As a result, my wrapping was always sloppy, haphazard, and improvised. I've even used duct tape to seal up a torn wrap from time to time. I look at it this way, why go to a ton of trouble for wraps that are going to fly off boxes in seconds and be forgotten? Yes, yes everyone made fun of my wrapping, but I never cared. Now, since I give you cash, usually there is nothing much to wrap. An envelope, a tag, a gift bag, and maybe a bow, and I'm done, which creates more time to drink the can of beer for the tree.

Putting my inner Ebenezer aside, what I still love about Christmas is seeing you in my home and the family get-togethers we always have. Such things are the real gifts one gives and receives at Christmas. When you are a kid, there is magic and excitement in the air during the holidays. Santa Claus, presents, and things like school plays bring something larger and better than everyday living into your life. As you get older, those things get more routine. At least they do for me. The magic I felt when I was young faded away long ago. But when we are around the tree or the table at Christmas, the magic comes back for a while. Seeing you smile and have a grand time takes me back in time, and I remember what this time of year has always really been about. It's about **us** and **not** the stuff you see. That is the true joy of Christmas for me.

Xmas with MeeMaw

To Roger and Jane:

In contrast to my meager efforts to get into the Christmas spirit, MeeMaw usually did the opposite. The tree was full of ornaments, there were lights on it, and had a real star on its top. The den and other rooms had a host of little Yuletide knick-knacks, like little Santas and elves, ornaments, and snowmen—sometimes an extra small tree, too. The presents were painfully and properly wrapped, and they were piled high around the tree. When Granddad was around, sometimes they put up outside lights, too. Plus her cooking efforts doubled at that time of the year. She made fudge, other traditional Christmas candies, and the always popular and tasty baklava. MeeMaw always made Christmas a big deal for all the people she loved.

As far as gifts went, she did not just get something for everyone that was easy or trendy. MeeMaw always had a knack for getting everyone things they would really like or really wanted. Even the surprise gifts were like that. No bottle of cologne or perfume from her, it was always something neat and unusual that appeared out of the gift wrap. The combination of getting things that were totally unexpected with some you did made the usually short and predictable gift opening something special and memorable year after year.

A lot of people go to such trouble because they feel obligated to do so or for show, but not MeeMaw. She did, and still does, those things for one reason alone. That simple but shining season is her love of family. That has always been her way. When I was a little kid, it was no different than it is now. The only difference now is that since she lives in an apartment, she does not have the space for all of the stuff she once put up. But some of it still comes out of her boxes stored in her closet to adorn her place. While her life's circumstances have changed, some things like Christmas have remained mostly as before, which is a key to remembering the past.

That shows us that tradition and family are why Christmas is special and lives in our heads during the year. What a family does then really defines who they are. The times we spend together, and more importantly **how** we spend them as one, paints our family's portrait. The many special things MeeMaw always does for us all means that picture is a pretty one to behold and is brighter than a thousand Yuletide trees with their lights.

Jeffery W. Turner

One Xmas at Granbury

To Jane:

Do you remember one of the Christmases in Granbury? One in particular is still sharp in my memories. That Xmas was the first time we went through the downtown park with all of the lights on the trees and the library that had been turned into a giant, indoor Xmas diorama of sorts.

I remember one night before Xmas when we went walking around the park. The city had trussed the trees with bright strings of lights. The lights hung from the trees in the park, casting warm and soft white light over its grass, playground equipment, and all who walked through it that cold night. The only thing that would have made it more magical would have been the presence of some snow on the ground, which, of course, was very unlikely. The city of Granbury does this display each year, and that year was special to me because all of you were there with me looking at the lights. Like most young boys, Roger was not so engaged by it, but you were. You looked at it with glee, while he walked through the soft glows more stoically like me. But what really got everyone's attention was what they did to the inside of the library. That sight made both of you kids take notice and me as well.

And what did the library do? Most of the inside of the building was turned into an indoor winter wonderland. Little dioramas, masses of decorations, nativity scenes in miniature, a forest of Christmas trees, and little Christmas towns adorned the place. They called this elaborate production "The Enchanted Forest."

I remember everyone walking around the place, marveling at the details of the exhibit. You could have spent hours in there and not seen all of the minutiae contained on the tables and shelves. All of it was draped in white tree flock and lit by candles and flickering lights, giving the library a soft and shadowy glow. All in all, it was a big place filled with Yuletide glee, built with a horde of small and beautiful things.

But what was most magical to me was the look on *your* face. You were perhaps eight or nine and immersed in what you saw and were fascinated with the many small things surrounding you. You walked around in quiet, wide-eyed wonder at the huge panoply of holiday objects around you. Your brother liked it, too; but being a boy, he was not immersed in it as much—his mind was perhaps on other things like the unwrapped presents and gifts at the house.

But yes, that look of little girl wonder on your face was something that still shines bright like the lights in the park did that cold, wintery night. Christmas is a bright and magical time of the year, filled with family ties, gifts, and other delights. But the real present that night was seeing your face: happy and filled with delight, as you walked through an enchanting place with your brother and me. You as a little girl lost in wonder at a joyful place during a happy time of the year is still a bright Christmas light in my mind even now.

Watching Cartoons with Roger

To Roger:

I recall my dad watching cartoons with me on Saturday mornings, as I have noted above. We would watch Bugs Bunny, the Roadrunner, Daffy Duck, and Foghorn Leghorn and laugh and grin. Your granddad thought they were as funny as I did. You and I did the same thing as father and son, but boy-oh-boy have cartoons changed between my childhood and yours.

The old Warner Brothers 'toons had the humor of the World War II generation through them—in many ways the humor was for the adults more than the kids. It was not racy or sexual; but as a grownup myself, I realized later whom the cartoons were for, and it was not just the kids.

So when you were a little boy, we had the same experience with cartoons as my dad and I did. Instead of Warner Brothers, we watched Beavis and Butthead, the Ninja Turtles, and Ren and Stimpy. These modern cartoons were very different from the old ones. They contained material that was unthinkable a few decades ago: mentions of various bodily fluids and organs, sexual innuendo, and other topics that would have made The Beaver's parents die of a heart attack. But I liked them as much as you did because I admit I enjoy such stuff. As Beavis so eloquently said, "***My bunghole will now speak.***" This quote says it all about those shows.

Over the years, we sat in the den, watched them, and laughed. Your favorite was the Ninjas, I think, and mine was Beavis and Butthead, closely followed by Ren and Stimpy. Regardless of our specific favorites, we did this over and over, like so many dads and sons do. I know I watched cartoons and shows with Jane too, like the dreaded Barney mentioned above in another Note; but I do not remember doing that as much with her as I did with you. Who knows? Maybe it is more of a father and son thing to watch cartoons where, "***Hehehehe ... fire is cool,***" or "***Poor Steeempee was tortured and eeeea-ten,***" or the Roman god of the porta-potties on Beavis and Butthead declared His Anger at the sinful mortals who destroyed His Temples, the port-a-potties. Yep, maybe such things aren't really for the girls.

Some years later, those shows became no more. Like any TV show, they never last forever and are replaced by something else—their more memorable moments still remembered by their fans of old. No more Beavis, instead, you saw Sponge Bob and others of that sort. Time moved on.

When you were a teen and young adult, we did not watch cartoons because you outgrew them, of course. But sometimes we still did the same thing, watching weird movies together when you were over. One example was the comedic flick, *Vampires,* starring James Woods. We both truly loved that movie's off-the-wall themes, like the Catholic Church sponsoring vampire slayers and the priest watching the slayers get drunk while chasing the whores bought with Church funds. Another one was *The Sopranos*, with all of its dark humor and violence galore. Our kind of stuff, eh? Indeed so.

In that way, things moved full circle. Something we did when you were a kid was something we did again when you were an adult. Just like me and my dad did. So it was *Back to the Future* in a way. But that film, its themes, and offshoots are another tale left to tell. As always, the past becomes present—what once was, is now the present and beyond. So it will be with cartoons and fathers and sons.

Notes To My Kids: Little Stories About Grown Up Kids

Swimming in my Pool

To Roger and Jane:

When both of you were little, we spent a lot of time with MeeMaw and Granddad Tom in their pool in Gainesville. On many hot afternoons, we were in that big, grand pool, splashing around and diving into the deep end. Your grandparents would hold you when you were little and could not swim on your own. Later you were wrapped in a life jacket when you could float without them always hanging on. I was there, too, as were your mom and cousins. But most of all, I remember the joy you had with them on so many days until MeeMaw sold the house after your granddad died. Many good and wonderful memories came from that pool with everyone there. They are still in my mind and in the pictures of you two as well.

Those fun and happy times lived on with me over the years. Many times I would think back on what we did in that pool and wish they would return. Of course, I would have to buy a house with a pool to make that wish come true.

When I was looking for my current house, I looked at more than one, none of which caught my eye or interested me even some. But when I saw the Aransas Trail house, I had to buy it. It wasn't just the game room or the beautiful park down the hill, but it was as much the pool in the back. I instantly imagined us in that pool, splashing around and having some fun, just like we did when you were little in Gainesville. I bought the house, which I am still in today, and waited for the hot summer so we could all get in.

And that we did. That first summer, now eleven years gone, was spent in that pool. You were bigger then, but it was still like before in a way because all of us were in a pool. We would swim around, Jane would sunbathe, and Roger would dive in. I would guzzle some beer, and you had some cokes. We snacked on some chips and swam around some more. After getting waterlogged and sunburned, we would get out and dry off and return at night or the next day in the sun. Once more on those days, we were in the water having some fun. Each summer we got in was just like we did before at Gainesville and that long-gone pool.

Now that you are grown, we don't get in the pool as much as we did. You both are grown and not over as much these days. The pool is still there, the pump is always on, and the water swirls around the kidney shaped sides in silence most of the time. If my pool was like a person, would it be lonely without us in it? Would it be sad without all three of us swimming around?

Being there alone, I wish you two were there, but I try to not get lonely because I see a day when you two will be back as before. Not just with me, but maybe with a spouse and my yet- to-be-born grandkids. Maybe one day hence, when I am old, there will be some little ones in my pool with me, just like you were with my dad and me. That way the flowing water of the stages of our lives will circle around and find us gathered together once more. That way, the pool won't be lonely anymore and be filled with a laughing and splashing family once again.

Wolf Calling in Fort Worth

To Roger and Jane:

One weekend when you came to my house in Fort Worth, we did something my dad and I did when I was a kid. We went wolf calling. Wolf calling, you say? There are no wolves locally. True, but there are lots of coyotes, and that is really what we went to call one evening.

After telling you we were going to try wolf calling, attracting them that is, I identified a place not too far from my house that looked like good ground for this endeavor. There were three hills covered with post oaks and bordered by an open pasture that was being graded for new houses. In fact, I had seen some coyotes there in broad daylight when I went walking up there. There was a small creek to the southwest of the hills that I guessed the coyotes used for water. You could get into the area since was no a gate and the dirt "roads" in the construction area were well packed. So after buying a wolf caller, a device used to make the sounds of animals that would attract the predator desired, we were ready to go. So one cool and moonless fall evening, we drove up there and started to call the coyotes.

We sat on the tailgate of my pickup, the dear old F150 I had for so long, and I started making the squealing noises my dad had showed me how to do long ago on my granddad's farm near Valley View. To see the coyotes, we had a large flashlight with red plastic taped over its end, so we could cast light on them without them seeing the beam—coyotes are supposed to be color blind—thus, the red plastic used.

I kept the calls going at irregular intervals, just as my dad taught me, paused, and shined the light around where I thought there would be coyotes. Like so many times when I was a kid, there weren't any to be seen.

Yes, many times no coyotes will appear when you call them, even though they are nocturnal creatures; and many times are not very scared of humans. But that night, they were elsewhere or *were* scared to come out towards us.

While we wanted to see the local cousins of the domesticated dogs, we were not successful. But the result was not what was really important. The real result of that night together was being able to do something with you that most urban dwelling kids never heard of, much less had the chance to do. Thus, we did just that, and I also got to remember similar fun nights with my dad that had happened decades ago on a hillside pasture near the two stock tanks on dark, cold nights on my granddad's farm. I hope one day you will recall that night with the same fondness, and maybe even try it with your now unborn kids. Perhaps, you'll have better luck than we did, and the coyotes will come out for you on that night to come.

Jeffery W. Turner

The Aliens at Aurora

To Roger and Jane:

In 1897, it is said that a UFO came flying low over Aurora, Texas, hit a windmill, and crashed, casting wreckage over several acres of farmland near the town. Supposedly, the body of the pilot of the alien saucer was buried in the cemetery there. This series of events was even reported in the *Dallas Morning News,* which still publishes to this day. In the present time, this purported "Texas Roswell" has been investigated, but no set of data or facts has emerged to prove or disprove the story absolutely. But the general opinion is that it was a hoax of some kind, perhaps done to save the town of Aurora, which was shrinking in size.

Regardless of the truth of the matter, we went up there one weekend with MeeMaw to see the site and the cemetery. Aurora is not far from Fort Worth, being just west of Rhome, which lies on highway US 287.

Aurora, itself, has few buildings, and one could make the case it is hardly a town. But the story of the UFO looms larger than the city limits do, and we arrived there one afternoon.

After exiting 287 and arriving in Aurora, we went to three places. The cemetery was first, the hilltop where the UFO supposedly crashed was second, and the UFO gift shop, painted green like an alien, was the last.

At the cemetery, a state historical marker about the incident explains the story and talks about the UFO's pilot being in an unmarked grave. We entered the graveyard, which was covered with oak trees, and looked around its grounds. I had seen some information in a book that discussed possible locations of the alien's grave, and we went to those places and looked around. We didn't solve the mystery, so we then went up to the hill, where the stories say the spacecraft crashed.

Right by Highway 114, which bisects Aurora, we went up a road to the top of a low lying hill, where a couple of houses stand. You can go only so far since there are fences and gates around the homes. If you did not know the story of the UFO, the scene could be anyone's rural abode: no historical marker or shrine— just houses, outbuildings, equipment, and some junk. No sign of a long, downed saucer was seen.

We went back down the hill to our last stop in our investigation: the green UFO museum and gift shop. It is a small house by the road, mere yards from the supposed crash site. We parked and went inside to look at their wares. On its shelves, one saw UFO books and VCR tapes— this was a little before DVDs were the rage. Of course, there were toy aliens and UFOs as well, plus some arts and crafts for the not-so-extra-terrestrially inclined.

But one thing did catch my eye that I bought for Jane. That thing was a drawing by a local artist that showed a cowboy pointing up and shouting a dire warning about things coming from the sky to Aurora. To me, that was the most unique thing in that entire green structure. We took it home, and I had it framed; and for a while at least, it hung on Jane's bedroom wall, but I do not know where it is now, I am afraid.

But whether or not that neat picture still exists, tucked away in some box of half-forgotten mementos, is not important really. What is important is the fact that stories come down to us from the past to be considered in the present. These tales can be myths, something historical and real, or a story like Aurora that is somewhere between fact and fiction. Spending time together to see if they are real is the big discovery to be unearthed, you see. Going to some slightly out of the way place to see something new or strange is an expedition well worth the time. Especially, if one's companions and crew are not a bunch of aliens in an UFO, but instead are the ones you dearly love.

Jeffery W. Turner

My Recipes for You

To Roger and Jane:

As you both know, one thing I always loved doing when you were over was cooking you a good, homemade meal—a feast of good things you liked. Of course, the things each of you liked were always different.

Roger was always more like me. You would eat and like just about any type of food imaginable: from BBQ to sushi to German to whatever. It was all destined to enter your hungry mouth to be swallowed. Now Jane, you were, until somewhat recently, the complete opposite. Your meal of choice had a consistent menu: homemade chicken nuggets, corn, and mashed potatoes—and cream gravy, of course. You two were culinary opposites, for sure.

Since I cooked so much, just like my mom always did and still does, I began writing down my recipes to put into a book for you two and maybe for someone who might be willing to buy it, too. Over time, I came up with stuff that tasted good, so I added it to my book. Why did I do this? Because your grandmother made something like that for your aunt and me. She made notebooks that contained many of the favorite dishes she cooked when I was young, plus one of the things her mom, my grandmother nicknamed "Muh," made in a separate notebook. Since these dishes and the family meals around them always meant a lot to me, I wanted to leave you the same legacy—a legacy of good food and good times together.

That way, you could one day point to some recipe in the book and tell your offspring, gathered in your own kitchen on some holiday or family occasion, something like, "Yes, I remember one winter day when your granddad made his turkey chili for us."

Thus, the tradition that has arisen in our family of good meals shared by the clan on special days will continue. One generation sharing its stories with one another, all centered on the simple act of making something good to eat for the people you love and

Jeffery W. Turner

care for, will carry on down the long road of time of our lives.

Your Christenings

To Roger and Jane:

Your mom and I were raised in different religious faiths. She was Catholic, and I was raised in the Church of Christ. The Catholic faith was an ancient institution, whereas the Church of Christ originated in the 1800s and was fundamentalist in creed. When I was in high school, our family ceased attending—our lifestyle was perhaps not as fundamentalist as the church desired; and hence, we were going to Hell since we danced, drank, and swam in mixed company.

On the other hand, your mom's family kept going to church at least somewhat regularly. In short, your mom was still a practicing Catholic when we married; and while I never converted, we agreed you two kids would be raised as Catholics. Being someone who is not strongly religious, I had no issue with that.

One side effect of that joint religious decision was that you would be christened as required by the Catholic

Church. Again, I had no issue with that since I hardly ever went to church, had already been baptized, and believed there was more than one way to attain salvation. Hence, one of the Fathers sprinkling you kids with Holy Water and mumbling some Latin was fine with me.

After Roger was born and at the age required for christening, we spoke with one of the priests at Holy Family on the west side near where Grandmama and Granddad Harry lived and set the date for the event. This ritual was part of a regular Mass.

On the appointed Sunday, we dressed you in a little, special white gown and went down in front of the congregation during the appropriate part of the Mass. We took a seat, and your mom and I held you. I want to say you were quiet, slept, and did not cry. The Father and the altar boys went through the many faceted Mass rituals, and it was time for the christening itself. We and the other parents were called down to the altar by the priest, arose, and went down there with you. I don't remember what was said specifically, or even if it was in Latin, but I remember the sprinkling of the Holy Water over you and the other babies. It was over quickly, we went back to our place in a pew, the Mass resumed, and was over. Afterwards, we had lunch together and it was done. We went back home after a while and another Sunday was over.

Five years later, it was your turn, Jane. I think you wore the same little gown that had previously adorned Roger on his day. We got up one Sunday, returned to Holy Family once more, went through the same rituals, the same prayers, saw the same Holy Water get sprinkled, and it was over. Both events were short and sweet, as you can see, but were important to your mom and her parents in many ways.

Time went on, years passed, and you two went to Mass with your mom over in Plano. Your mom decided to become Methodist and left the Church since no parish near her was likeable. No more Mass, no more priests, and no more Holy Water were in store for you two or her. But even with none of us being part of the Church now, these memories still remain. Well they should since while we may not go through the doors of a church much now, the times spent there are important and should not be forgotten. The stories, the rituals, and the teachings of faith are some of the things that define our place in life, tell us whom we are, and provide our proverbial moral compasses. Hence, when I hear something about the Catholic Church on the radio or TV, I am reminded of you two as babies at Holy Family Church and how significant that was. Those little drops of Holy Water and those days still flood my memory now.

You Babysitters

To Roger and Jane:

When we lived at the Monterrey House, we had babysitters who kept you after school and in the summer when school was out. There are three that I remember the most, and this is their tale.

The first and perhaps the most important one was Leslie Graves who lived near us by Loop 820. Leslie kept Roger at her house for quite a while. She had a few other kids she kept and was a young mother like your mom. She was about our age, was easy to talk to, and nice. Her routine was pretty simple during the day. Watch TV or Disney movies, play some games, and view some cartoons in the afternoon while having a snack. Roger liked her too so we knew he felt comfortable with her. At some point, she and her husband bought a new house and moved away. We lost track of her, so where she is now is unknown. Wherever she and her family are, I hope they are well.

Then there was Miss Millie – I finally remembered her name. She was a grandmotherly old black lady who lived not too far away. She had a kind voice and did not anger. She really did treat Roger like a grandkid I think – this was before you were born, Jane. Each time I came home before your mom, he seemed to be happy and always had a smile on his face – unless he was sick, of course. She would recount what games had been played or told us about pushing you on the swing out back, then off she would go at the end of the day.

Finally, there was Meerna who kept you both. She was an Iranian girl who studied at UTA. She was smart, pretty, and took to you both. You liked her too, and your mom and I thought she did well with you even with your difference in age. I can picture her in my memories now, she had dark black hair, medium skin, and I will admit a nice, curvy figure. But looks aside, she was a good caretaker of you.

Now those times have past, and I admit there are a lot of details I have forgotten. But you should remember them; after all you were around them more than I was sometimes. Babysitters are one part of growing up that you should not forget. I remember some of mine too. For example, I remember one old lady, Miss Pierce, who kept me and your aunt – we still tell MeeMaw about the time when Granddad and she were in San Francisco, and Miss Peirce, who was keeping us, dribbled salad dressing on her blouse from a salad we were having. Now that might be considered cruel to recount such a thing about a very kind lady who kept me, but it still sticks out in my mind.

The point of that is I bet you two have some funny stories about your babysitters tucked away, too. They are there alongside the ones that show you that these same people cared about you enough to spend much of their days with you.

That shows you that caring about someone means you might be remembered by someone you have not seen for decades. Because they were good to you, they should not be forgotten. So always care about those around you, and be good to those who in turn care for you—it's just the Golden Rule at work in your lives each day.

Notes To My Kids: Little Stories About Grown Up Kids

Christmas at Grandmama's and Granddad Harry's

To Roger and Jane:

Your mom's parents always did Christmas right. While they were in an apartment not a house like my folks, there always was a large and intricately decorated tree in their living room, lots of presents for all of us—but especially for you two—and a big Christmas dinner or lunch with some drinks. It was a big production on a small stage.

Grandmama ran this show of course; Granddad Harry was mostly a spectator to all of this. Grandmama would spend a great amount of time decorating her tree. Hours in fact. Since shopping was a favorite past time of hers, she spent many hours at Ridgmar Mall and Hulen Mall to find everyone's gifts. Like your mom and MeeMaw, she also spent hours wrapping the gifts or sometimes had them wrapped at a store. Such things made up her Christmas preparatory ritual.

When we knew we would have the "tree," we would drive over to their apartment at the appointed time. Once there, the dinner and present opening was done almost like a ritual. It was that way because your mom's family was much more formal than mine. An effect of the culture they grew up in in Mississippi. Everything had to be done a certain way, it was just how it was, and there was not much deviation from the past.

We would first have some drinks, usually liquor not beer, served in Grandmama's nicest drink glasses with a napkin wrapped around their curves. Then we would eat the meal, which was always an oven roasted turkey, mashed potatoes, and the-always-asked-for-green-bean-casserole, covered with the canned and crispy fried onions of course. Finally, there was a store-bought dessert since Grandmama did not cook much. Another drink or two was consumed as well.

The grand finale was opening the gifts, especially for you who always wanted that first. Grandmama would hand out the gifts, the wrapping paper would fly off, and soon their living room floor was covered with toys, discarded gift boxes, and the shreds of the once shining gift wrap paper.

We would sit around and look at you two playing with your gifts, at least the ones we did not have to take home and assemble, and then it was done.

As with all such events, we would load up our car, hug everyone bye, and Grandmama always made a point of wishing us Merry Christmas as we left for home. As I said above, the way your mom's family did things was more formal than mine, but it was still a time for the family to be under one roof for a meal and a good time. Such things are what bind us together over time, the source of many good memories that define our era on this orb and whom we are. More importantly, it shows us that every family has different ways. That difference, while sometimes a source of friction, should be considered something good for us all. Because of these differences, you will create your own rituals down the line for your own special days to come.

Jeffery W. Turner

Swimming at Grandmama's

To Roger and Jane:

During the summer, we would go over to Grandmama's to swim at her apartment's pool. Your mom and I would get you into your swimsuits, grab some floats and toys, pack some towels, and off we would go to the west side of town for the afternoon.

Once we were there, we would make some drinks, juice normally for you two or a Coke, beer for me most of the time, and perhaps a Crown and something for your mom and Grandmama. We would go down the stairs and set up on some chairs by the pool, hopefully in the shade. Before we got in, we would whip out the sunscreen and cover you up. Your young skin was easily burned and a sore little kid was not something good to behold. Finally, on went the floats to keep you safe. Then we were a go and in the water we would go.

We would splash around, swim, and carry on. That went on for a while; sometimes a long time until we were wrinkled and soaked. Depending on what time of day we were there, you would get a second coat of sunscreen too. Your mom did the same, but I hardly ever used the stuff, being darker skinned than her.

Then we would get out of the pool and dry off. Sometimes, we would change you back into your clothes and dry your hair. You didn't care much for that and wished you were still in the water outside. On some days, we stayed for lunch or dinner. Regardless, at the end of the day, you were both worn out and went to bed tired.

There were many days like that over there. When I am on I-30 and go past the exit to Ridgmar, you can see the apartments where we went. Other places from those times are around too, like Holy Family Catholic Church and the building where Grandmama worked for many years at NTS. Going down that road and seeing those places seemingly unchanged is like rewinding your trip down the road of life. There are many stops along the way, and hopefully, those stops are good. Grandmama's pool *was* a good place to visit and stop driving for a little while, both literally and figuratively. It was a wonderful milepost to mark our long journey through life by.

Working at the Rent Houses

To Roger:

When I was growing up, Granddad and MeeMaw owned six rent houses in Denton. The houses were wood-frame homes in older parts of towns. Most of them were near the universities and the renters were students.

When they bought one, we spent a lot of time fixing it up so it could be rented. When rented, your grandparents would collect the rent, fix things, and evict non-paying tenants. On most projects, your aunt and I were put to work doing a variety of things at the rent houses and was something we never liked. These unwanted toils and projects were a regular part of growing up.

After you were born, your mom and I did the same thing and bought two duplexes in Arlington near the UTA campus. Later on, I turned the Monterrey house into a rental as well. When your mom and I divorced,

I received and kept up the houses and managed them myself. Thus, the routine became part of my life too as an adult.

When you got older, I took you over to the houses to help me out. Maybe you were too little at first, but my dad always took me, many times on Saturday mornings when I wanted to be watching my cartoons at home. While I always did the "heavy" stuff, sometimes I had you do something small, like pick up the trash. Sometimes, Jane was there, too but at the time, she was too young to do much. Like me, you never liked going to the rent houses very much. I guess what kid would? In fact, one time we really got into a bit of a fuss about doing rent house chores and that was not good. But luckily, a solution arose to this problem after that time.

When we moved to Gainesville when I was a teenager, Granddad and MeeMaw sold all of the rentals to a man who was the scout master of my scout troop at one time. The deal was done, and there were no more trips to the rentals on Saturdays—a happy result for me. I did not miss them at all. A blessed relief had been found to the chronic ill that had beset my free time.

Likewise, while I had the Monterrey house until 2006, the City Of Arlington bought the duplexes to widen Center Street near UTA and downtown. I was out of the rental world for the most part then. You never had to toil at those places again.

Now, Jane, you, and I went to the Monterrey house a handful of times, like the last time we were all there after I sold it; but neither you nor your sister had to endure doing such things again.

Looking back to my growing up years, I realize that my dad was not just trying to make me work; he wanted to be with me and also teach me some practical things. Teach me he did because when I had my own rentals, I already knew how that business was done. Perhaps some year hence, you will look back on these days and realize I was doing the same thing as Granddad Tom. Just having you around was a good thing. But if you learned something along the way too, then your rent into adulthood was also partially paid. That bill was well worth paying on time.

Notes To My Kids: Little Stories About Grown Up Kids

Jess and Madge

To Roger and Jane:

At the Monterrey house, we knew our neighbors and liked them with the exception of grouchy, old Mrs. Shaw to our west. The neighbors who were our most loved were, of course, Jess and Madge Moore to our east. That retired couple was a shining example of how neighbors should act to each other. I think you both would agree.

Jess and Madge were from the World War II generation. Jess, who Madge called Jimmy (his real name was Jessie and should not be confused with our other neighbor across the street named Jim Moore), served in the U.S. Army Air Force in England as an aircraft mechanic on B-17s, and had stayed in the later separate U.S. Air Force and worked on the big B-36s that were made in Fort Worth after the war. Later, he became a Fort Worth city Marshall until he retired. Madge was a typical housewife of that time. She cared for their kids and tended the house they lived in. As far as I know, she never worked outside of their home like most women of that time. As an aside, Madge's first name was Robbie (Madge was her middle name), which I never heard anyone use.

All in all, they were a typical *Leave It to Beaver* couple of the "Greatest Generation" and its age. They had a home and a modest income, plus by the time we showed up on Monterrey Drive, several grandkids as well.

But their ordinary life was not what made them special. It was their friendship and willingness to help. Jess was always someone you could talk to, as was Madge, although she was a bit "gripey" at times. I can remember many times trying to fix something, and Jess would lend a hand to show me how to do things I found impossible to master and do well. He did other things like letting me borrow tools to fix something at the house. Madge would sometimes give us advice on things and was around as well. They were like a lighthouse in the fog of life, a beacon certain and sure, unfailing in their presence.

The other part of why we liked them so much was the interest they always took in you two kids. He was like another grandfather to you both. When we were outside, he would always talk to you, ask what you were doing, and how your schoolwork was going. When you weren't nearby, he still asked how you were. Without exception, he was curious about your lives. Madge was curious, too, but we saw more of Jess thinking back over those years now long gone.

As the years went on, Jess and Madge were always there and part of our lives. After I moved away, I sometimes saw them when I checked on Monterrey, which had then been rented out. They never seemed to change much. It seemed we were the ones that had become different, especially since we had all moved away.

As Jess got older, he got a little fuzzy, maybe it was just old age or maybe it was Alzheimer's. He was not as sharp as he was when you were little. Madge seemed to be the same, albeit of course acting older, since they were both in the 80s by then. You can't be the same forever since time always marches on.

Then in 2005, I found out Jess died. I could not go to the funeral because I was away doing the project in Austin, but I sent some flowers to the family. It was the least I could do given all that he had done for us you see. His passing was more than just a man dying; it was truly the end of an era, as the cliché goes. It was the closure of a chapter in our lives that in many ways seemed idyllic and unchanging.

Time of course has marched on, and after I sold the Monterrey house, I seldom went over that way. Sometimes I drove by our old house to see how it and the neighborhood were doing but I never saw Madge again and I don't know if she is still alive.

But one day I did get a glimpse of her, not in person, but in the images of the digital cyber world. Do you remember the time I found the picture of her on

Google Earth? She was standing on the northwest side of their house, looking at the Google car with its cameras. She had a dour look on her face, and I'm sure she was wondering what the heck that weird looking car was doing driving down Monterrey Drive. The familiar unhappy look on her face made me think of several things at once. Like the many times I had stood in our yard talking to Jess and hearing her call out sharply to him, demanding even, saying "JIMMMMMYYY!" I imagined we were still there, seeing him go off to tend to her like we had never left the old house and them.

The memories of them should stand out for us all. Their nature as good and steady neighbors should make us hope that wherever we live in our lives, we will have such good people close by. A good neighbor is hard to find these days where the people around our homes are unknown or impersonal entities at best most of the time.

So in the days yet to come when you move into a house of your own on some quiet, tree-lined street, think back to when you were little on Monterrey Drive. You should remember Jess and Madge fondly and hope your new neighbors are like them. If these new folks in your lives are even a fraction as nice as Jess and Madge both were to us as a family, you will be greatly blessed and made richer as a person indeed.

Your Friend Curtis

To Roger:

Everyone has a best friend or two when they grow up. You do things together, like play or go to school, and become inseparable in some ways. Then they go their own way and life goes on. This was the case with you and Curtis, your friend from Sycamore School.

Sycamore was a great school for you given your premature birth. Your teacher, Mrs. Travis who is in this book too, taught you well and cared for you greatly. She also taught your friend Curtis who was autistic, unlike you. For whatever reason, you and he hit it off. I am not sure why, but you did – why do any two people become friends? We also got to know his parents, the Air Force doctor from the base and his wife from San Antonio named Pilar. I thought his dad was funny; I remember his darkly funny story about the "Chamber of Horrors" exhibit at the pathology lab at the base. Its artifacts were objects "extracted" from a certain orifice of airmen at the base. That grossness aside, he was a funny and good man who we saw at the school.

You and Curtis had the usual sleepovers and such. He was more reserved than you, but he was always well-mannered and behaved. I do not remember you two fussing like most friends wind up doing and moving apart. But with your more dominant personality, you were the leader of the pack that was you two boys.

While you were at Sycamore School and afterwards, this friendship went on and was good for you both. This relationship furthered your development as well because it increased your social skills. I could see Curtis getting better, too. Not just from being around you, of course, but see it we could. Even so, he lagged behind you due to his condition. Regardless of that fact or any other preemie-related things, you two remained good friends.

When your mom moved to Plano, you lost touch with him. Time and distance are never friends to friendships. With our ever mobile society, such things are more common than in the past. Gone are the times when most of us have friends for life.

In spite of such things, he **was** your good friend, and you are better for that former bond. Over time, look back on him because his friendship was a priceless thing to have. Having a good friend is a rare and great treasure many never see. I can still recall his shy, little boy smile and his quiet, pint-sized voice. You should do that, too—be glad he was in your life, and gave you gifts you never knew he gave.

Jeffery W. Turner

Al and Anita and Branford, Too

To Roger and Jane:

Back when we lived on Monterrey Drive, a couple, Al and Anita Morrell to be exact, bought Jim Moore's house after he died. They were an African-American couple about the same age as your mom and me. They later became our good friends.

At first, Al and I started chatting while we worked in our yards. We would mow, trim, and then meet on one side of the street or the other and drink some beer. We would swill our suds, cuss, tell gross stories, and talk about a lot of things. Sometimes Jess would join us, too. Al and I always got along, and I enjoyed our times outside with some cold brew.

One time, I invited them over for dinner and your mom just about had a cow. Being from a part of the country where the races did not socially mix, she just about blew a gasket—the culture she came from was the source of this angst. She sort of got over that and

Al and Anita came over, we sat around our table one weekend, broke bread, and had some drinks. In the future, we went over to their house too, but your mom never fully accepted them even though she was always friendly to them both.

Al and I were pretty close, and your mom was friendly with Anita, but they were never really close friends. Regardless, he and I always talked, even though we both knew of your mom's out-of-date predilections towards race.

Later on, Al and Anita had a little boy whom they named Branford, who was younger than you both. Both of you liked the little guy, but I seem to remember Jane enjoying playing with him the most. As time went on, we saw him grow up; just as we watched you two get bigger. Certainly the stages of life were at work right before our eyes.

When your mom and I got divorced and I moved back into the house, Al and I were still friends, but things were not totally the same. Al and I still drank our beer out in the yard, but I did not see Anita much after that point. When couples split up, something in that social fabric is torn, even amongst those who remain nearby. Once that seal is ruptured, it is never the same. And thus it remained until I moved away not long after that.

I saw them now and then when I went to Monterrey to collect the rent. But I lost track of them after they too split up, moved, and sold their house. Once I looked Al up and found that he had moved to Arlington and lived not too far away. I also found his phone number and left him a message or two, but he never called me back. To this day, I do not know why. This shows us how friends come and how they go. Sometimes they come back, too. Few people you meet will always be your friends. People have their own lives, and what they want or need alters. Thus, what seems like an eternal flame might eventually die in the winds of change. So while Al, Anita, and Branford also came and went from our lives, I am glad they were there for a time and will always remember them well, as I walk down the road of my own ever-changing life.

Postscript: I recently got back in touch with Al via Facebook, and it was like nothing had changed. We had a cold beer together, too.

Tom and Carol

To Roger and Jane:

Another couple your mom and I were friends with was Tom and Carol Cobb, who lived on the edge of Saginaw and Fort Worth, not so far from where I do now. Carol used to work with your mom, and that was how we met.

Tom and Carol were interesting folks. I do not remember much about her background, but Tom's was that of a master car mechanic you might recall. Your mom and I always had Tom work on our cars. We would take them to their house, and I would watch Tom ply his trade while we drank beer. One funny thing about Tom was he liked to watch porn while working on the cars. He had a TV out in the garage, looking over the tools. Half-naked gals in beer posters covered the walls, where his tools were hung. He would put in a VHS tape and then the madness would begin. We would slurp on our beer, watch wild sex acts, make gross comments, and laugh all while he spun his power tools and pulled out some car parts. He explained he could watch the flicks out there but never inside where Carol was. It was one of those quid pro quos most couples have. You can have some fun, but not all of the fun you might like to have.

Carol was a very a nice lady. She was down to earth, just like Tom, and you could see why they got along. She was more of a white collar professional by trade than Tom, but she was certainly no Highland Park snob either. She could solve a customer's problems and then have a big drink and a cig. In some ways, she was like you mom, you see. She would work hard and play hard all in the same day. She and Tom also had a huge collection of movies on VHS tapes – not his sex tapes I should point out—and was one of their big common interests. Carol spent a lot of time with those and her other hobbies, while Tom was out in the garage with the cars and his own tapes mentioned before.

While their kids were much older than you are, Tom and Carol still knew you well. As often as not, you went with us there. You liked them too and never seemed to mind going over there. Of course, Tom's tapes did **not** get brought out when you were around, but that never mattered because you kids always had a good time.

Once your mom and I split up, I did not see them much anymore. When I bought my current house, I went over there a few times, and it was like old times again: the porn, the garage, and the beer. But after a point, I lost track of them—travelling, girlfriends, and the changes of life flowed forth once more over me. Even so, I sometimes saw Tom driving your mom's old black convertible he bought from her at some time. I can recall one time in particular when I was on Basswood about to go west over the bridge on a spring day, I saw him turn north onto I-35W with the top down and his hair in the breeze as he gunned your mom's old car. Certainly that scene could have summed Tom right up—a man and his favorite toy out for some play. That was the last time I ever saw Tom.

You kids told me they moved to Sherman for Carol's new job. But even now, I still think of them. In fact, I used to drive to work down Mark IV Parkway which went to their house. As I drove south on Mark IV, I would see their house on my right. In my mind, I could see us there too. Your mom would be in the house with Carol having a drink while, Tom and I, along with his porn, were out in the garage guzzling down some cold beer. If you kids were around, no dirty movies would come out. We'd eat dinner, watch a movie, and then go home with a fine evening done. What could be better than being around good friends and those that you loved? Nothing much can be better, that is for sure.

As a result of those good times, and as I have written about other friends above, I remember Tom and Carol fondly to this day. We are truly blessed when we have people like that in our lives. They were good friends to us and great people who I **thankfully** think about

Jeffery W. Turner

each time I go down Mark IV to who knows where in my own little life.

Seeing Harold Taft

To Roger and Jane:

Besides folks like Jim Moore, Jess and Madge, and Al and Anita, we had other neighbors when we lived on Monterrey, like the Jeffries, whose kids played with you, to the locally famous weatherman, Harold Taft who lived one block up the street.

Like many people from here, Harold Taft was a well-known and well-liked, if not loved, public figure. He was a true pioneer in television weather forecasting. Many people took his word as weather-law. I never watched other channels, instead I watched **only** the old WBAP Channel 5 to hear him every day of the year. I was a true follower of "His Truth". Do you remember me joking he was the "Weather Pope" and making the "Sign of the Radar," mimicking the Catholic sign of the cross in jest? Most assuredly, I was his acolyte and disciple at all times.

All TV personalities have a human side, what you see on air is not what is seen when off of the air. Harold was no different. Sometimes, I saw him when I was out walking for my diabetes. He went walking for medical reasons, too because he had a heart attack once. I would talk to him briefly, and off we would go. Some of our neighbors spoke to him, too. More than once, I saw him across the street with Jim Moore (not Jess Moore, remember), chatting away. Harold was friendly, but not overly so. He was a serious professional and that showed up in his demeanor to his fellow citizens at times.

Harold also had a "crusty" side let's say. One time when he was talking to Jim, I was there too. He described in some detail how "some son of a bitch" tried to run him over on Meadowbrook Drive. He said that with a devilish grin and that was that. Seeing him on air you might think he drove to the station in some boring, large family car. Not so, no station wagon for him. Instead, he had a little Honda CRX that he drove or rather sped, I should say. Many times, I looked out the house's front window and like clockwork a little before 5:00 pm, you would see his CRX literally ***zoom*** down the street going to Broadcast Hill. He was a conservative man, but not entirely so.

The years went on, and even when I no longer lived on Monterrey, I watched him every day. At some point, he got cancer and became very ill. You could see the progression of the disease wear on him each day. His delivery was not smooth and seemed to be confused some too. But Harold Taft was no quitter, and on he worked. But he worsened and eventually went off of the air, just a few weeks before he died.

In this day and age, folks on TV seem to come and go like the changing of the wind. They appear on the tube, stay a while, then get fired or move on to some other town never to return. But Harold never did that. Maybe it was a different age or time, but he was in front of our eyes almost every single day.

That should tell us to look down the long road of time and not be so set on what is right here and now.

Harold did that. He stayed in Fort Worth, did the weather for 40 years or so, and did charitable things that were larger than his own life and self. The number of people like me that he informed and helped is beyond counting. For those things he is remembered as a legend by countless citizens to this day and was loved and admired when he was alive.

We should all hope that we are remembered that way too. So be like Harold Taft in your own lives. Be consistent and constant in your efforts, be friendly to your neighbors, and make someone laugh. Or maybe tell someone the weather forecast for the day, and see what good things come back your way somewhere down the road.

Notes To My Kids: Little Stories About Grown Up Kids

Swing Sets and a Tree House

To Roger and Jane:

When I was growing up, we had a swing set or two, but not a tree house at our house. A cousin or two had tree houses which I always loved to be in. When you were little, you had both of those things in our big back yard. My parents gave you a nice swing set one Christmas, and Granddad Tom built you a little tree house of sorts in the big oak tree that was the center of our back yard. You had before you your kingdom, a fun place for play that was in and under that large and beautiful old tree.

Under its branches, we spent many an hour, on many a day, playing together. At first it was just Roger, but later both of you were there. Your mom and I would swing you back and forth, and you would go down the slide. You would be in the tree house, too, which was really a plastic playhouse propped up on some stilts. Fill it you did, smiling all of the time on endless sunny days that you hoped would never end. Like when you were in your rooms playing happily with your toys, seeing you around that big tree was a magical thing to behold.

When your mom and I split up, the swing set and tree house were no more, at least not at the house. I think your mom took those things with her. Then the space around the tree was just grass and a bare spot, where the swing set used to be. The shade was still there, but not you or the things you had loved so much.

But that should not make us sad because the happy days spent under those big branches still make me smile. Seeing you in my mind, still very young and not dealing with the things you do now as adults, brings good feelings into my heart every day of the year.

The house and the big tree are still there. I hope whoever lives there now has a swing set under that big, old tree or a tree house up in it, and their days under its wide arms are filled with big, innocent smiles like ours were on those warm days long ago.

Jeffery W. Turner

The House on Monterrey

To Roger and Jane:

While it has been a long time since we lived on Monterrey Drive in east Fort Worth, that house and neighborhood still have an important place in my memories. To me, it will always be your childhood home, even though you both left there for points east with your mom. For whatever reason, that little house still looms large in my mind.

I could probably write a book all to itself about it. All of the things I remember from when you were around me every day and how that time was in my life always come back into my memory. Like when I drive on I-30 back home from Dallas, I see the names of the streets on the bridges over the highway leading back to our old neck of the woods. While I can't see the house from that vantage point, I can see the times spent there in my thoughts.

Little and big things both fill my mind about that house. From the type of trees it had (like the big oak tree in the back to the two pines in the front) to the shape of the rooms inside of it— remember the big den/dining room through the middle of it? Plus the many events that took place there over the years, like your birthdays, the times spent in the back yard, and when your grandparents came over for the holidays.

Your mom and I thought the house looked like something on the old *Leave It to Beaver* TV show, a program that showed a rather idealized version of family life. It may have been an unrealistic point of view, but it is one many people identify with in our culture to this day. It was a view of what a family should be like and how it should live.

And maybe that's what I am thinking too when I see that forever white, two-story house with the dormers and its trees inside of my head. Perhaps I want to paint an idyllic picture on top of life's ups and downs, which is the real canvass we see ourselves on each day.

Regardless of why I feel that way, or why I still hold that old house so dear, I know that it is good to have such a place in your life; a place that can be an anchor in life's always present storms and gales. A place that as we get old, we can think back upon and remember times that were memorable and good. A place we can still call home even though we are far from its safe and comforting shores.

Gifts You Gave Me

To Roger and Jane:

Christmas in our culture, while once mostly religious, is now more about gifts than anything, except maybe the family times spent together. Parents and grandparents give the kids gifts disguised as being from Santa, until some older kid tells them that Mom and Dad are really Santa, and no one really comes down the chimney. Also, that Mom or Dad actually eat the snacks left by the fireplace for the Big Guy in Red. On the other hand, the kids give the parents some gifts too, usually assisted by the parent's spouse or someone else.

When you were younger, this was the case. Your mom did this even after we divorced—and MeeMaw, too. MeeMaw or Mom would take you shopping, and they would pick something out that they thought I wanted or needed. Over the years, these gifts were a variety of things—many of them practical. Pajamas, kitchen stuff, a book or two, and other things were laid out by the tree for me to open up and see.

As you got older, I sometimes told you something little to get for me at that time of the year. That is something I still do, as you know. Even so, you two would surprise me with something else too. Maybe you still had some help, especially from my mom, but the result was the same. A gift from you was always a wonderful thing for me every time.

Some of those gifts were simple things. Like one Christmas, you gave me two large coffee mugs, one of which I still have. It has a stylized chef on its side with a checkered pattern circling around. Actually it has the word "soupe," not coffee, on its rim, but I always used it for a cup of Joe or hot tea in the morning. Seeing that years old and battered mug, its twin was broken by accident years ago, reminds me of you and those gift giving times.

Sometimes, I get sentimental about those little things —and not just Christmas or birthday gifts. Like the two plastic drink mugs I have from one of your fundraising efforts when you moved to Plano with your mom. I still have them and use them. Even though they're red, white, and blue Lone Star State design has faded with time, I could never throw them away because they came from you.

You can see I keep little things most people might have chucked because they have a big place in my heart. I have been that way my whole life. These treasured things, some from my childhood and my mom and dad, fill my house, boxes in my closet, and drawers in my desk upstairs. The course of my life is laid out in a trail of little things. While these things are small, their memories are large, especially the ones from you, whom I miss not seeing every day.

So when I give you something little, hold on to it, put it safely away in a box, or stick it up on your shelf; so one day when I am gone, gaze up at it and think of who gave it to you. Let those small things be a big reminder of me, who I was and how much I loved you both.

Jeffery W. Turner

My Cheap Xmas Trees

To Roger and Jane:

Each Christmas at my house, I seldom put up any decorations or lights, but I always put up a Christmas tree for you two kids—albeit a very cheap one most years. Indeed, I was never one to decorate much for Christmas, or any holiday for that matter, unlike MeeMaw or Stephanie did.

When the holiday season arrived each year, I drug out my old, fake tree; set it up someplace; and decorated it. Decorate might be a charitable way to describe what I did to my tree because it usually did not take me more than a few minutes from start to finish to complete that task.

I kept the adornments for the yuletide tree simple. I put hanging ornaments on it and some strings of garland, too. I seldom put on lights and never once flocked a tree. The one thing I usually did after a point, and maybe the one specific thing you and others remembered me doing, was what I used for the star that went on the top of my plastic tree. That object usually consisted of an empty beer can as you know. I did that with your mom once as well, much to her displeasure, but I have done that more than once in my own home over the years.

Sometimes, I used a can I hungrily drained while decorating the tree or when I wrapped your presents in my crude and sloppy way. MeeMaw and others always commented on my rather rudimentary wrapping jobs. But regardless of the brand of brew consumed, a bright shiny aluminum can became my personal Star of David, which brought me some yuletide glee. Glee albeit induced by the ethanol in the beer, you see.

You might ask why didn't I adorn the pointy top of my tree with a nice and appropriate ornamental star? Using a can was a bit of humor done to make MeeMaw, or others like your mom, squawk. While I never thought of it when I did that, I can say now it should be a reminder that Christmas should be about each other and not the many gifts or even the symbols of the holiday. Forget about the pretty presents and instead, look around at **who** is by our tree, not **what**.

In that way, a simple can of beer on top of a Christmas tree can remind us of our greatest gift. Our love for each other is the thing we should treasure and hold most dear each December 25th.

Your Pets

To Roger and Jane:

Like most kids these days, you had your favorite pets: dogs, cats, and some other things, too. While pets come and go, you had a couple of special ones that even I, who usually never has a pet, still remember you enjoying.

The first special pet we had was Mary Jane the cat. Mary Jane was a black kitten with a white stripe on one side of her face that your mom got somewhere, maybe the pound, but I do not recall where now. Mary Jane also had a sister, whom we named Alice, whose markings were a true mirror image of Mary Jane's. Yes, Mary Jane and Alice to use the old name-based cliché. We thought having two twin kitties would be neat. I always liked cats, and they liked me, so I was okay with that.

Very quickly, our desire to have two cats did not turn out well. Alice was sick—she could not go to the bathroom much at all. We knew something was wrong with her. We took her to a vet, and he examined her. He quickly determined the little cat had a congenital birth defect in its digestive track that prevented it from having a normal bowel movement. In fact, he picked her up and squeezed her to make her go. Alice would surely die soon, he said. With sadness, we put her to sleep. I can still remember the little cat on the table at the vet's office before he put her down; it was a sad, but necessary thing to do, because Alice was suffering so.

Now Mary Jane had quite the opposite life experience, as you know. She lived until she was quite old, blind, and feeble; and she passed when you two were in your teens. Before that time, she was a big part of the house and our lives. While your mom kept her as part of the divorce that was okay because she was really for you kids. She was a good cat and she was certainly loved. I liked her too and as you will recall, I would try to pet her when I came to see you. But over time, she forgot whom I was and would not let me pick her up much—and later, not at all. Oh well, cats are like that sometimes.

Now Beau the dog was another matter. I am not a big fan of dogs in general, but Grandmama got him and brought him to us. He was named Beauregard or Beau for short. He was a smallish dog with long, scraggly hair. He was friendly, playful, and not mean at all. However, he tore things up in the back yard, which did not sit well with me. Because getting rid of him would cause a problem he stayed around. Even though I disliked him, I still petted him some. I may not like dogs, but I am not cruel to them. Even so, they are troublesome, drooling creatures I do not want to have around with a few rare exceptions, as you know.

Poor Beau, like Alice, did not live very long. I remember Roger calling me in tears saying he was dead. Roger found him dead as a doornail in the back yard. To make a long story short, it was determined he died from the pesticide I put out in the back yard to keep the bugs out of the house and ticks away from you kids when you were in the yard. To be specific,

Diazanon was the chemical I used. For the most part, I was not very sorry he was gone, but I could see how sad everyone, but me, was about his death. The poor mutt was certainly loved, and I remember how you two played with him and that he loved you both back.

Beloved pets are one of the things that make growing up special. The animals that are part of the family give you love, fun, and good memories to treasure as you get older. Even though you get new pets as the old ones die or disappear, the ones you had when you were little will always have the most special place in your heart. I still recall my favorite pets, too. Yes, even I, the dad who has no pets, once shed a tear when a pet so loved passed away.

Making You Stuff

To Jane:

Moms and dads always help their kids make stuff for homework assignments or things to play with around the house or yard. Your mom and I were no different and constructed various objects for you and Roger. With the passage of time, most of these things fell apart or got torn up and forgotten. But some of them managed to survive physically and are still remembered. While I know we built things for Roger, none of his objects seemed to remain, but at least two of yours did. This note is about them, plus a swing I built for you once upon a time.

One thing I made was the grey elephant. You were at Harrington at the time and had some animal-oriented project to do, I think. One weekend when I had you kids, we went to the store, Wal-Mart probably, and got some Styrofoam balls, wooden dowels, and other supplies from the craft aisle to build it with.

I painted one big ball for his body and a smaller one for his head. I made legs and feet with dowels and ears and a snout with some type of wrinkled plastic tube. Plus, he had craft toy eyes that would wiggle around a bit. When fully assembled, he was around eight inches high and stood up on his own.

You took him to school, and I guess you got an A for *your* work. It is funny how kids get the grade when the parents do the work; I guess teachers know that and don't mind that fact. Regardless of who actually made him, the little grey elephant was a good looking project I must say and as far as I know, you have him at your mom's. His slightly unrealistic stance and his big black and white eyes are still clear in my memories, regardless of where he is now.

Another project we did was making you a guitar. This project took a little more work but turned out well, too. I nailed two pieces of wood together to make the rectangular body and thinner neck of the guitar which was painted purple. Next, I cut plastic lines to make the strings; each was a little longer than the others, so they each had a unique tone. Shiny, silver screws were emplaced to hold the strings taut so you could strum them and make a tune of sorts. Finally, I found a white strip of something, which became its shoulder strap. When all of that was done, you had your guitar, slung it over your shoulder, and began to "play" it.

You really liked it, and I remember you "playing" it while listening to songs and pretending you were a pop star with a big hit on the radio or MTV. As I type this, I can see the guitar in the southwest corner of your room. It sits there quietly now, not being played, but I can picture it in your hands as a fired-up little girl like it was yesterday.

The final thing I made for you was the swing at one of my old houses. Since there was no playground nearby and you loved to swing, you made your request known. I found the parts for a swing and strung the thing up on the branch of the tree on the west side of my yard. You swung back and forth many a warm day while I watched from the patio nearby. A rain or thunderstorm was about the only thing that stopped you from using it most days—and some not so warm days because swinging was something you loved. Sometimes, you made me push you on the swing, like I did at the beloved "New Park," now so far away. A simple thing like a swing provided many fun times for both of us.

Simple things, yes, simple things are sometimes more than they appear to be. At the time, they appear and get used, and their value is not immediately seen. But because most things come and go, what usually remains are their memories in our lives. Yes, some of them linger like your guitar; but most of the time, only the far-off echo of their existence hangs on here in the "eternal now."

Even today speaking of "the now," I remember some things my mom made me when I was little. One very bright memory is the space station I had her make, the one from the movie: *2001: A Space Odyssey*, which is still a favorite movie of mine. She made it with cardboard and tape, and I played with it until it fell apart and was destroyed. Little kids can be tough on even their favorite toys, you see. But even though that thing built by a loving mother is gone, its memory remains, a lighthouse pointing into the ever-darkening shadows of fading remembrance.

Now that you are grown, look around my house and your mom's, too, and seek out the things that we made for you. Pick them up and think back on how happy they made you feel. Keep them if you can, but always store the pictures of them and us in your mind, so you will know what to do when your own kids ask you to make them things some day.

Jeffery W. Turner

Lullabies

To Roger and Jane:

Besides reading you bedtime stories, your mom and I would sign lullabies to make you sleepy. There were several of them, but there were two that were my favorites. The songs were the old and familiar, "Rock-a-Bye, Baby" and "Hush, Little Baby" that countless parents have intoned to their kids. Sitting in the rocking chair, I would hold you up against my chest with my arms around you and start signing. I would never make it on *American Idol,* but as far as I know, babies don't care about parents having a bad singing voice.

Here are "Rock-a-Bye, Baby's" lyrics:

Rock-a-Bye, Baby
Rock-a-bye, baby, in the tree top.
When the wind blows, the cradle will rock.
When the bough breaks, the cradle will fall.
And down will come baby, cradle and all.

This little tune is simple, and the verse repeats over and over and over. The cadence developed while singing its gentle words makes a baby feel at ease.

But my real favorite was "Hush, Little Baby." It has more lyrics than "Rock-a-Bye, Baby," and I repeated its verses over and over too until you fell asleep. Maybe my wretched voice did not distort its calming and soothing words.
Here are its lyrics:

Hush, Little Baby
Hush, little baby, don't say a word
Papa's gonna buy you a mockingbird.
And if that mockingbird won't sing,
Papa's gonna buy you a diamond ring.
And if that diamond ring turns brass,
Papa's gonna buy you a looking glass.
And if that looking glass gets broke,
Papa's gonna buy you a billy goat.
And if that billy goat won't pull,
Papa's gonna buy you a cart and bull.
And if that cart and bull fall down,
you'll still be the sweetest little baby in town.

I wonder if you have any memories of me singing these songs to you. You heard them when you were very little, but maybe you heard them so much you might have some faint memory of their sounds—a faint and distant sound of your dad holding you close.

Whether or not you recall these lullabies aside, why is writing about this important you ask? The answer is pretty simple. These songs were part of your daily routine when you were very little and the act of singing them while holding you close was an act done out of love for you. Plus singing those ancient tunes was one way of caring for you when you could not care for yourselves.

Caring for someone when they can't care for themselves is the main point here. When you are born, your parents have to care for you. But when you get very old and feeble, your kids may have to care for you. Life is a cycle: the roles are reversed, and the caregiver becomes the one cared for sometimes. Now having said that, if I wind up in a nursing home one day there is no need to sing lullabies to me. Just being there with me and remembering my love for you will be comfort enough if I get into such a state. If you do that, the care you were given when you were little and helpless was worth every single syllable that I sang with my ghastly voice those many nights and days now long ago.

Jeffery W. Turner

Fever and the Bathtub

To Roger:

All kids have a fever now and then, but you were sick more often than other little ones. You would get fussy, and we would check if you had a fever. Many times, we could simply put our palms on your forehead and immediately tell if you were too hot. Other times, we took your temperature. When you were little, we used a rectal thermometer, which is not a fun thing to do when you are old enough to know what that is and use it. When you were older, we had a regular thermometer, which was more pleasant to use.

Once we saw what your temp was, the first thing we did was give you Children's Tylenol – how many bottles of that did we go through with you? That would usually get your temperature down, and we would take you to see Dr. Scroggie the next day to see what you had. If your fever did not come down, we would call an off-duty nurse and ask her what to do.

We were told to resort to more drastic measures then. What procedure did we do to get your temp back to normal or something closer to the Holy Grail of 98.6 degrees Fahrenheit? A bath was it, nothing more than that—a mostly effective cure for your fever.

We would fill the tub with lukewarm water and lay you on the large sponge we bathed you on. Your mood would not be good, and you cried because the water was not as hot as a regular bath. We got a smaller sponge or washcloth and washed you down, concentrating on your head, which was the hottest part of you. This would go on for a few minutes then we got you out, dried you off, wrapped you in a towel, and checked your temperature again. If it did not go back down, the process was repeated to see if that helped.

Most of the time, the bathtub trip did the trick and got you cooler with some help from the ever present Tylenol, too. When you were cooler and your temp stayed down, we would put your pajamas back on, lay you down in the bed with us, and try to go to sleep.

Most of the time, the ordeal of the bath and the effect of the Tylenol made you calm, and you went off to dreamland. But sometimes, you were still fussy, and we would sit in the rocker and sing to you until you finally closed your little eyes and slept. Then off to Dr. Scroggie when the morning came to get you totally well.

We did this routine with your sister, too, but not nearly as much as we did with you. You won that undesired contest, if you will. But crossing that health finish line did not get you a trophy or a prize. Instead, it was one of the many mileposts in your younger years that we all went by to see you grown and well. Now you have been sick since then too, like when you were in college, had pneumonia, and were in the hospital for a week. When I saw you so sick, I thought back to when you were in the NICU, and wished some Tylenol and a warm bath would make you well. I couldn't do that, but my mind went back to when I did that since it was so much a part of your past.

Sometimes, we can't personally heal someone we love who is sick. But sometimes, we can. A small thing like a bath can go a long way to make a child feel better. That is a lesson you can apply to your entire life, regardless of being sick or well. A small act of kindness performed for someone loved will have a lasting effect. Medicine for one's soul, I think some say. Remember that and always be ready to give someone dear to you a bath of love when they are feeling the harsh heat from the hot and wearisome fevers in their life. By doing so, the warm bathwater and Tylenol of love will heal their ills.

Jeffery W. Turner

Riding Segways in Austin

To Roger and Jane:

One of the favorite things we ever did was ride the Segways in Austin the Thanksgiving I was working there on the Carlton-Bates project. I do not remember how I came up with the idea to do that, but I wanted to do something other than just walk inside of the capitol's dome downtown or go have nachos at the Oasis on Lake Travis with you. So we rode the Segways, and it was a fun time indeed.

Over the years, I had seen the Segway "vehicle" on TV, but I had never seen or rode one. I remember talking to the place in Austin that gave the Segway tours of downtown and asking questions about them. I asked if they were easy to ride, how hard it was to balance them, and if teenagers like you would enjoy the ride. Since the answers I got were acceptable, I made our reservations for the tour.

That Thanksgiving was a bit hectic if you remember. I came home to Fort Worth, and it was my turn to have everyone over, so I was busy getting the smoker ready for the turkey and the ham. We had everyone over and you two spent the night. We got up the day after Thanksgiving and drove to Austin and left our stuff at the extended stay place I stayed at. The next stop was downtown and the Segways.

We parked on the street, and we walked into the shop and gazed at the odd-looking devices, which looked like an old fashioned pogo stick with two large wheels on the bottom. We checked in and got trained on how to run them. Then we departed for our short tour of downtown Austin that cool and cloudy day.

We started down the street in a line; there were around eight of us in total and a guide. We quickly got used to driving them and how they steered. It really became a very easy and natural thing to do, like riding a bike or driving a car. None of us wrecked or hit something, which was good.

Over the next couple of hours, we road down by the Colorado River and the streets of the southern part of downtown and went by the State capitol building. We snaked up and down the little hills and wound our way back to the starting point where we reluctantly parked our two-wheeled steeds.

After our ride, we ate lunch at the Texas Chili Parlor, which unfortunately was not so good, and toured the inside of the capitol. Of course, we went to a store by UT to look at T-shirts and saw the football stadium too. It was a fun day in more than one way, one grey and cold but filled with the warmth generated by the fire of being together and having a good time.

And so it was that day and weekend. On Sunday, I drove you to Austin's Bergstrom airport to fly back to Love Field, home, and your waiting schoolwork. On Monday, I went back to work there in Austin.

That was one of the most fun weekends I had with you two after you were grown. Riding the *Segways* was a *segue* in life because I started to realize more and more that you both were no longer little kids. In that way, driving the Segways that day was like driving down a new road in the way I saw you two: a new highway of our lives that we were driving down, still together, even today.

Jeffery W. Turner

Seeing Owen Roane

To Roger and Jane:

By now I think you know I think family is the most important thing in life. Not just one's parents or grandparents or aunts and uncles as well, but also the members of our extended family, too. By that, I mean people that are even second or third "this or that's", too. One of those "this and that's" was Owen D. "Cowboy" Roane, my grandmother Turner's cousin who would be my third cousin.

Owen was from Valley View, like the rest of the clan. But unlike many of the family members he was not a farmer. He retired as a school administrator, but his real claim to fame was his service in World War II. During that all important war, he flew Boeing B-17s over Western Europe and flew on raids that are now recorded in the history books, such as the infamous "Black Thursday" raid over Schweinfurt, Germany, where the USAF had its highest single raid losses of crews and planes in the entire war. Amidst that carnage, he was not wounded and later flew all of his 25 required missions and returned home. He stayed in the Air Force after the war and reached the rank of colonel.

Many men served in the Air Force in World War II, it was the US *Army* Air Force then, but relatively few got their picture in history books. But Owen was one of them who did; he is in more than one book on the strategic bombing campaign over Europe in fact. I have one of them, called *Flying Fortress*, and there he is sitting on the wing of one of his B-17s with a big grin on his face. When I was a kid, I did not realize he was part of the family but when I was a grown man, that changed. When you kids were a bit older, I thought you should meet him given his status as a World War II vet and his presence in the books. Hence, I contacted him and his wife and we up drove to Valley View one Saturday to see him.

You have to understand something before I go on. To your generation, World War II is something in a history book or on the History Channel. To mine, it is much more. When I was a teenager, many of the men that fought in that war were middle age and were all around you. In fact, one friend's dad, Stan Hicks, flew B-17s in Europe like Owen did. Stan was not alone, you see. There were millions like him. Thus, while these men did not talk about the war much, it was still real enough to those around them merely because you knew they had done their service.

If you remember, when we talked to Owen, he really did not describe any details about the combat either—few veterans ever do—instead, he talked about related things, like his old commanding officer the famous/ infamous—which one depends on who you ask—General Curtis Lemay. Do you remember his story about how LeMay griped out Owen and his crew for "being out of uniform" when they were taking a bath in a stream in North Africa after one of the so-called "shuttle raids"? Or telling us about how the book, movie, and later TV series, *Twelve O'Clock High,* was based on the famous 100th Bomb Group, "The

Bloody 100th" that he flew in? That one of the characters in the book and film was based on him? I think I know which character it was; there is a young lieutenant from the south whom I think is him. He would not say which character was him if you remember; I do not know why, but I am sure he had his reasons for not confirming that to us.

And finally, we talked about the gorgeous art print, "Scaling the Alps," hanging in his house that shows four B-17s flying over the Alps from Germany to North Africa—one of which is his. I loved that picture; and as you know, one signed copy hangs proudly in my game room for all to see. His signature is on it too, along with some of his crewmates'.

Like I said, we did not talk about the combat and death he saw but talked instead about things that surrounded those horrors now decades past. Such was the tone of the two hours or so we spent in his home by I-35 that day. It was a very important day for you. You got a glimpse into history and heard about people and things, like General LeMay, from a perspective few get to see. The fact that he was family made our visit and talk with him more special.

Therefore, when you see an old B-17 at some air show, think about your cousin Owen, your fourth cousin I might add, at the controls almost half a century before you were born. Think of him and his fellow men-at-arms and be proud of what he did for our country then. Show his picture to your kids one year hence. If you don't, ***I'll*** pull out my books, including the self-published book Owen wrote of his time in the war, and do it ***myself***! Maybe writing does run in the family, eh?

Notes To My Kids: Little Stories About Grown Up Kids

Eating at Wyatt's Cafeteria

To Roger and Jane:

Do you remember eating at Wyatt's Cafeteria with your mom and me? You should because we did it so many times when we lived on Monterrey. On some days when we were tired or did not feel like cooking, we loaded you in the car and drove up Sandy Lane, then down Brentwood Stair, and then a short bit on Handley to Wyatt's, which was next to our bank in the building where your mom worked after she left Dillard's at Northeast Mall.

We parked the car, piled out, went in the door, and got in line—it's a cafeteria, remember. Your mom and I picked stuff out for you when you were really little; but when you were older, we let you choose what you wanted. Also when you were really little, you would be placed in one of their high chairs of course. Your mom and I got grown-up food—I liked the fish, the chicken fried steak, or a veggie plate. I don't really recall what you mom got though. We paid and then proceeded to a table, unloaded our plates, and started to eat.

We got you kids going first. One thing we did when you were little was cut up anything that required a knife, like a piece of chicken or meat. If you had a roll, we split it open and buttered it and of course, opened up your carton of milk or juice as well. Once you kids were eating away, I would find myself some hot sauce or clear pepper sauce, which I used to douse everything on my plate. Yes, I know I still do that; I haven't changed.

We ate our meal, talked to you, made you mind when you acted up, and sat for a bit. When done, we got up, left, and repeated the drive there in reverse to get back home.

You are probably asking me why I am writing about eating at a cafeteria, which is no longer there. I'll tell you, of course. When I was growing up, my parents took us to Luby's Cafeteria in Denton to eat, usually for Sunday lunch. To us, that was something special because back then people did not eat out like they do now. We did the same general routine after church was over. We would drive up Carol Boulevard, then west on University Drive, park, go in, pick out our food, and sit down together and eat. No more, no less than what we once did.

As an aside to you, Roger, the last time I was in that old Luby's was when your granddad was starting to get sick. You, he, and I went to Denton for some reason and ate lunch there. As before, and at the Wyatt's in Fort Worth, the food was plentiful and good. I even remember eating big lima beans and cornbread (soaked with butter and clear pepper sauce as always) as part of my meal. I don't recall what you and he dined on however. Regardless we were all there together—three generations of Turner men breaking bread as one. A simple meal but our gathering was special.

Such meals and times were something I always enjoyed, although now a cafeteria is an anachronism to most people. They are not fancy, trendy, or "hip" enough for those who are *cool* to be seen at. To me, that is a great shame. A simple cafeteria is a wonderful place for a family to go and eat. It has home-cooked meals, it's a friendly pace, and you don't have to dress like you are going to a bar either.

Not to mention the best thing of all—the memories one can get eating with those you love. That thing is a great and satisfying dessert not found on their menus but is there for all who enter a cafeteria's doors.

Learning to Drive Cars

To Roger and Jane:

What is a parent's worst nightmare? Their teenagers learning to drive a car. The parents know their children have to learn to drive, but they worry about wrecks, speeding tickets, and the higher cost of insurance is always present and greatly feared. However, the teenager views this as the first real step towards getting away from Mom and Dad's eyes and parental control. It is a true yin-yang event in modern life.

As all kids do, you both went to driver's education to learn how to drive. Once completed, you were given learner's permits and under Mom and Dad's right seat direction, you could venture forth onto the road. Since you lived with your Mom, she did more of that than I did. But I helped out some, too.

When you were over, we would climb in the truck and go out for a spin. Neither of you cared for my Ford

F150 because it was big and did not drive like the sedans your mom always drove. Regardless, we went out on roads away from town, where no traffic was seen. Thus, we *all* were safer than we could have been.

I remembered my dad and mom teaching me to drive. Granddad had a truck too, and I remember him taking me *way* out of town on some farm-to-market road north of Krum, where he made me drive his pickup truck. I was not so good on the brakes, or the pedal, which he scolded me about. As with your first road driving experiences, luckily there wasn't much traffic around. But through practice and getting admonished a lot, I got the hang of it after a while.

You two were no different in that. Jane picked it up quicker, but you both got the feel for the road. Sometimes we drove around parking lots too when not many drivers were out. Perhaps the reason for this choice was there were fewer things for you to run into and damage when we were off of a road. No one ever got hurt on your training runs, I might add.

Then the magical day arrived when you got your driver's license and you could go off on your own. While this is great fun for the teenager, it makes the parent's stomach turn as I hinted at above. The worry over the driver's permit is bad enough; but when you can't see where your kids are going or how they are driving, the level of worry goes up and up.

In the end, however, both of you never had anything really bad happen while driving. Yes, both of you had some speeding tickets and some small fender benders over time, but never a major wreck or incident. Thank God, unlike so many other teenage drivers we both could name.

In ages long past and in cultures now gone, children became adults in many ways. Boys became warriors and chiefs, and girls became mothers and matriarchs. Spears were chunked and enemies killed or rituals and incantations performed to mark someone's coming of age. In the end, I guess we are not different—the European-American culture has its rites, too. Learning to drive a car on our crowded and sometimes

Jeffery W. Turner

dangerous roads is one of ours. Learning to drive a real motor car is a big milestone on life's long and crooked road.

Breakfast with Roger on the Way to Sycamore School

To Roger:

When you were little and at Sycamore School on Fort Worth's southwest side, your mom and I took turns driving you to school because both of us worked a long way from there. Doing that every other day, I started a little tradition. On Fridays, we stopped at a Jack-in-the-Box on I-20 and had breakfast.

We would climb in my car and drive around the east side of town and onto I-20 and to Sycamore's part of town. We would pull into Jack, get out, and go in. A Breakfast Jack, some coffee or juice, or maybe a Super Taco was consumed. After we finished, we went back to the car and sped westward to the school. We would arrive, I hugged you bye, let you out, and inside to Mrs. Travis you would go.

That went on for quite some time, as you know. Each Friday, we did that as father and son, a little time together with you and me alone. A simple meal with just us guys—no girls were allowed. That is the way it should be because there are times for just a father and son. Boys love their moms, but a dad brings something only a man alone can show a boy. Maybe nothing macho or sexist, you see, but time spent with grown men shows a boy how to become a man.

Those little breakfasts were such times. We didn't necessarily talk about anything deep, after all you were in kindergarten and first grade at the time, but it was time well spent between you and me. It shows that a father and son don't have to do something that fits a stereotype, like going hunting or seeing some ballgame. In our case, that something was food. A love of good food and cooking is something we still share today and may have its roots from those days. Thus, lifelong memories and things we like to do together came from something as simple as having breakfast together on the way to school. Hence, while we filled our tummies with food from Jack on those days long ago, our hearts are still full from those great and *tasty* times.

Jeffery W. Turner

Roger and Terms Of Endearment

To Roger...

Most people have a favorite movie or TV show. I can remember my own favorites, some of which I still love as an adult, like *Star Trek* and *2001: A Space Odyssey.* You had, like most kids, an all-time favorite movie as a little boy: *Terms of Endearment,* which starred Shirley MacLaine, Jack Nicholson, John Lithgow, and others.

I really do not remember how you got so interested in that flick, which I liked too but you watched it over and over and over—never seeming to tire of its story and plot. That movie was not the type of movie most children would enjoy. There was no sign of friendly animals, superheroes, or kindly village elders visible at all. In some ways, the characters were quite the opposite of what would be seen in a kid's show. You had the main stars, Shirley and Jack, along with others, who were eccentric, somewhat lacking in morals, or simply colorful. All in all, it was an interesting and entertaining movie, albeit one with a sad ending.

While the ending was sad, it was still the story of a family. Perhaps the family element, even though not one cast from the 1950's *Leave It to Beaver* mold, is what appealed to you. Or maybe it was the little kids of the character Emma, whom you might have identified with. One day, I guess I will need to ask you why you liked it so much so I will really know.

Regardless of why you liked it, I grew to like it as well. How could I not enjoy it after seeing it literally dozens of times with you? I even ordered its soundtrack and enjoyed listening to it in my car while driving to work. What you the little son liked, so did the dad.

Perhaps, that is what I ultimately got out of watching that now decades old and mostly forgotten movie. That is, your children can expose you to things you never thought you would like. As parents, we try to do things with our kids to broaden their horizons. But this was a case where the total opposite happened—I learned to like something new because of you.

Fire Escape Plans

To Roger and Jane:

Do you remember that the Monterrey house had two stories and your bedrooms were upstairs? And that my current home is a two-story house with your bedrooms upstairs? Well, of course, you do. So what do you do in case there is a fire? You have a fire escape plan.

When you kids were little, your mom and I moved our bedroom downstairs once both of you were in this world. Before that, we were upstairs, and the bedroom downstairs was a guest bedroom. At that point, we thought through what do in case there was a fire to make sure you got out of the house okay.

We thought through all kinds of scenarios, like running upstairs to grab you both and dashing back down, or telling you to push out the screens of the dormer windows, go out through the window itself, and jump off the roof into our arms below. In the end, we settled on just running upstairs, depending on the situation because you were too little to follow complicated instructions, like going out through the dormers.

After I moved out of Monterrey, none of us were in a two-story house, and escape plans were simplified– just go out your bedroom window if there's a fire. But things change as you know, and I bought my current house –another two-story house with your bedrooms upstairs. So once again, I thought of fire escape plans.

My current house was very different than the old Monterrey house. There were no dormers and a roof to jump out to. If you opened your window, you simply had to jump; but there were bushes below. I pondered this problem and in the end, went back to the past for a solution and plan. To put it bluntly, I advised you to just run down the stairs, which were next to your rooms and go out the front door. As a last resort, open your windows and jump. Not much different than the old Monterrey plan, eh? Nope, it was really the same old fire drill.

This small story shows something obvious that has become a cliché. The more things change, the more they stay the same. Indeed so, and it also shows us to keep it simple (stupid), the so-called "KISS" acronym, which is another widely used cliché in many settings like business today.

But there is truth in both of those concepts. When things get complicated in your lives, or things get tough and hard, the solution to difficult times most often is something tried and true and not at all new. Just taking a deep breath, waiting, and thinking back on what has happened before will open a door to safety in your mind and away from the bright fires of adversity flaming around you in the present.

Jeffery W. Turner

Cutting through the Country

To Roger and Jane:

One thing Granddad Tom liked to do was drive through the country. MeeMaw said he was happiest while away from town and on a farm or pasture. A part of this was driving, when possible, down some farm-to-market road to places like a large city such as Fort Worth. I can remember many times when we went to eat at Joe T. Garcia's on the north side and got there by going west to Krum from Denton, and then south on FM156 all the way to the restaurant, which is just off Main Street (which 156 becomes). That used to drive me and your Aunt Terri crazy. We thought he should use the newly constructed I-5W, which had no traffic on it. But he did not many times. When grown, I did the same thing with you when we went to Granbury. Like Terri and I, you two never liked doing that much.

We did use the highways most of the way actually. We took 820 around the west side of town, and then down 377 to Wheatland, which is called "Whiskey Flats" since it has liquor, beer, gas, strippers, and a porn store. I would make a left there and go east on FM1187 through the rolling pasture land. Next I hooked a right and went south on FM1902 until I went west on Winscott-Plover Road to Cresson (where a good chunk of the movie *Pure Country* was filmed). You might remember I have a Note in "Days Remembered" about that road and its magnificent pasture views. On we went on that road to the southwest—past cows and gas wells, but not many houses or people.

When we got to Cresson, I made another turn. I went to the east on Texas 171 to a County Road near the border of Hood and Johnson Counties. On the way, I loved seeing the views of the wide vistas with Comanche Peak on the horizon far away. Such things made me feel alive and happy—there was more to be seen than what was in our neighborhood back in town.

Next, we went through the farm and ranch lands there to FM4. Then, we went west on 4 for a short bit, then turned south onto what eventually turns into Fall Creek Highway, which ultimately goes to Acton and Granbury. Fall Creek is a lovely place too. I have described it elsewhere in this book as you will read. What you see changed from open pastures to the "country-suburban" landscape that you see all around Granbury. Ultimately, we got to go where we wanted to go—Granbury, Acton, or Pecan Plantation.

To this day, you don't like going that way, even to your aunt's, which is just off Fall Creek Highway. This route was much more involved than the one Granddad Tom took to Joe T's that I hated as a kid. But like him and his love of drives through the country, I loved every minute of *this* drive with its many pastoral and far-off vistas.

What you two need to keep in the back of your minds about this tale is that one day you, too, may find your *own* country roads to torture your kids with. With that, another family tradition endures.

Uncle Mike Dies

To Roger and Jane:

After losing your grandfathers, Uncle Mike's death was an unexpected tragedy. He came down with skin cancer, which he apparently tried to hide, which spread through his body. After seeing Granddad Tom slowly die of cancer, this filled all of us with certain dread. We knew he would not make it and we braced ourselves for the worst.

Mike was a hardworking man and did not give up on things that were hard in life. This behavior goes back to when he and Terri first married. He was working on the plant floor at National Supply's factory in Gainesville. A high school counselor we all did not care for told him he was not "college material." It seems he took that advice; but after marrying your aunt, that changed. He enrolled in college at UNT, where your mom, Aunt Terri, and I went (and where MeeMaw and Granddad Tom also attended). He chose computer science as his major and went on through to get his diploma, making good grades, too. When he got focused on something, he kept his nose to the grindstone as they say, until he got the task at hand done.

That determination was still seen in him while he was getting sicker. He did not stop working until nearly the very end when he felt so bad. I can remember seeing him on the couch at their house with a computer in his lap, toiling away on some program for the Comanche Peak Plant, where he worked. But he was looking very bad and getting thin.

After months of fighting the cancer, he lapsed into a coma like many cancer victims do. Perhaps that is a blessing, given the pain that they endure. I remember he was near death and Terri had him home. To make it easier to care for him, a bed was set up in their den near the kitchen and such. We were all there one evening when he sort of woke up for a bit. I was next to him and he rose up and looked at me with squinting, cloudy eyes. I tried to talk to him, calling out his name, but he did not seem to hear me and laid his head back down and closed his eyes. That night, he passed away and was gone.

The funeral was up in Gainesville at the Vernie Keel Funeral Home, of course, and was the usual affair that you might expect. He was buried at the Valley View Cemetery, where my grandparents and my dad also lie. I can still picture your aunt and your cousins there by the casket so sad. To this day, when another family member is laid to rest there, we sometimes go by his grave. I have also gone by all of the graves of those I still love and miss—my dad, Mike, Aunt Sissie, Uncle Billy Mac, and my grandparents, too. Some of my great grandparents are nearby, as well. All of them are buried within yards of each other, except for your uncle who is a bit farther away. Indeed, much of the family is at that little graveyard by I-35. You can see four generations of names on its headstones, counting Uncle Mike's.

In a way, while death has separated us from them, we are still together. Seeing the family's quiet graves makes us recall the life and times of those who passed before us and our time with them, too. Hence, as life tells us the stories of our lives, so does death. Together, that yin and yang of existence tells us whom we are and whom we have been as a family.

The Turner Extended Family

To Roger and Jane:

When I was a kid, our aunts, uncles, and cousins were close at hand. All of us lived within about a half an hour of each other. When we visited Valley View, we sometimes saw both sides of the clan, especially on holidays since the grandparents' houses were across the street from each other on Lee Street south of the square. At various times, we would spend the night at the houses of our cousins too. Our family was large, but it was close because we were in one location. When I was a kid, those bonds were very close and dear.

But our family has been a bit different. Terri and your cousins were not so close at hand and lived over an hour away from you and your mom and about an hour from me. It was a bit more work to see them than it was to see my many cousins years ago. Regardless of the distance, we did see them some. Sometimes, it was at MeeMaw and Granddad's house in Gainesville and those summer days by the pool. Or it was on holidays there, at my house, or your aunt's. You played with your cousins who are your age, or nowadays, have some drinks with them and "shoot the shit." You kids got along and did not fuss, perhaps because you weren't around each other that much. That remains true today.

Your Aunt Terri treated you well when you were around her. I can recall her scooping one of you up with one of hers out of MeeMaw's pool. Or the "mass diaper changings" we had when one set of you were at that age. Or her feeding you kiddos a snack, too. I can say that when we were all together, we treated you four kids like one big, common "herd." Herd in a good way, I might add. That is, we did not see one child or set of kids as better as or worse than the other. In that way, there was a type of kinder-egalitarianism amongst us.

In the present time, we are becoming ever more spread out as our lives change, and you find your careers and loves. Instead of twenty miles or maybe an hour, hundreds of miles separate us now. This is even more so with your cousins from your mom's side of things. Such distances make it hard to stay in touch and gather as one family like we did before. We still do it some, but it is infrequent at best, and it will be even more so as the natural growth of our family goes on.

Over time, each of you will become the nucleus of your own gaggle of kids, cousins, and the like. That is a natural thing and nothing bad to behold. Your extended family is an important thing in your life. It is one of the biggest things that tell you whom you are. Yes, I have said this before in my tomes, but it is something I feel strongly about—with families being so mobile and scattered, we have lost something important by not being around each other much. I cannot imagine my life without the memories from my youth about my extended family. You have heard many of these stories, but the thing you need to do is make sure you have similar tales, too. That is, try to spend time with your cousins, do something fun with them, and in years hence, recall it around the fire with your own kin someday. On a cold night, those tales of old will give you warmth—even on the most frigid days life offers.

Birthday Cakes I Should Not Have Baked

To Roger:

As you know, I am a pretty good cook. I can whip up a good meal just about any time and cook just about any type of cuisine you could want. But the one area of the culinary arts I am not so good at is desserts. A perfect example of this woeful shortcoming was when I tried to bake you one of MeeMaw's "Billie Sue Chocolate Cakes."

This cake, a childhood favorite of mine and one you also liked, was an old fashioned recipe MeeMaw made me (and others) when I was a kid. That cake had cooked icing made with Hershey's cocoa to produce a rich, dark, milk chocolate dessert that when done right was perhaps a "food of the gods."

But let me repeat myself, *when done right* is the most important thing to remember. When not done right, the result was a kitchen tragedy to behold. Yes, this is about a time when I did not do it the way it should have been.

You may now ask what my mistake was. It was a simple thing I did wrong, caused by my tendency to not precisely measure things when I cook. I usually "wing" measuring things, like the amount of spices to use The outcome, while usually good, is not consistent every time. The ingredient of the chocolate cake I did not exactly gauge was the one I should have measured exactly to be sure. That ingredient was the cocoa powder that went into the batter of the cake.

Instead of using what MeeMaw's recipe called for I added an amount of cocoa that could have made a bunch of cakes—not just one. I scooped out more and more cocoa into the bowl, and I mixed it up. The batter was very dark indeed, but I thought nothing of it at the time. What could be wrong with more cocoa? Next, I poured the batter into my cake pans, and in the oven they went. After a while, they came out, cooled, and I iced up what looked like a normal Billie Sue cake. But appearances were not the problem, it was the God-awful taste. I had used so much cocoa, the flavor was beyond strong, to say the least. Horrible is a better word to use, I must say. It was really bad, and we all knew it with our very first bite.

Therefore, that cake did not get consumed with glee like a Billie Sue cake should have been. I think it ended up in the trash because it was so outright wretched tasting to the tongue. Who knew what the reason was in the blink of an eye?

It was MeeMaw, of course, the Queen of the Baking and Cooking. Having made many of these cakes over the years, she asked how much cocoa I had used. I did not know for sure, so I just said "a lot." The result was a brief lecture by her on always **exactly** measuring the ingredients of a dessert. If you don't, a disaster is what you will get.

Since that day, I have taken her advice to heart, but I can't say that I have applied it either because I have never baked another cake. Instead, I have left that birthday chore to others who follow the baker's art.

Jeffery W. Turner

Most thankfully for those eating the cakes, I am sure you will agree.

Roger's PT and OT

To Roger:

Most prematurely born infants have some physical issue. The type and severity varies wildly, but it is a lot more common to see such things than not. Your experience was no different, and you had issues with your physical development and dexterity. You had trouble doing more than one thing a full-term baby picks up on its own. Luckily, there are solutions to these ills. In your case, the solution was occupational and physical therapy.

When you were born, we were told you would likely face these things. Over the first years of your life, you were evaluated many times by more than one specialist at the still existing Fort Worth Child Study Center off of Henderson near downtown. Your mom and I took you down there for more than one battery of tests and found out to no surprise that your development lagged behind. You always tested as having above average intelligence, so the physical things were the problem and not your intellect. This showed up in how long it took you to learn to walk and how well you handled things like a fork and a spoon. You simply needed some help catching up, and that is what we did.

We were referred to an office that did physical and occupational therapy, north of our old east side neighborhood in the Newell and Newell Business Park and next to the Trinity River by East Loop 820. Based on what you needed, you went up there twice a week for what seemed a long time. Your mom and I would cart you up there and they worked with you for an hour. One visit would be pure physical therapy (PT) and another would be the occupational therapy (OT). The PT was covered by insurance, but the OT was not. After your 100-page long and $100K hospital bill, you were still an expensive kid! But don't worry about that since we never cared because we loved you so. Still do, I might add.

The physical therapist worked with your muscle tone and your ability to move. You were in physical training like an athlete in a way. They moved your arms and legs in various ways and stretched you out. When it was OT day, you worked with everyday things like a spoon and a fork to sharpen your skills. This routine went on for a long time and did not change much. But we could see the positive progress because you were evaluated again and again at that office and at the Child Study Center.

Then, the treatments finally ended sometime before Jane was born. Looking back, all of the struggles we had with your premature birth's after effects seem distant. Maybe because you overcame so many hurdles and trials to be the young man you are today. Or maybe it's just the passage of time, and it heals. In any event, you *were* healed, and that was the only thing we ever wanted for you, regardless of the time and cost. Your PT and OT were but two small steps in that large and lengthy process that has made you a healthy and successful young man.

Jeffery W. Turner

Country Day School

To Roger:

As opposed to the almost idyllic experience we had with Sycamore School, the time you two were at Country Day was not so pleasant. At the time, your mom started working over in Dallas, so finding a school that met your needs, and Jane's, was not easy to find. After searching around, we decided on Country Day School in Arlington, which was a convenient drive and had programs you needed.

So at the start of the school year, you and Jane went there. Since it was a private school, you had to wear uniforms each day. You wore khakis, a white shirt, and a maroon sweater on top. I still have a picture of you two in that garb on top of the little bookshelf in my office. You are both smiling big, with you behind Jane. It is a wonderful little shot into that time.

Jane's teachers were Mrs. Bush and Mrs. Darcy. Roger's was Miss Tennyson. Above, I mentioned the wonderful time we had at Sycamore, didn't I? The time at Country Day, however, was not so wonderful, due to Mrs. Tennyson. Tennyson was a young, rookie teacher. We were assured she could handle giving you extra time and attention that was required. That she did, **but**. . . The "***buts***" were the issue with her. She was smart and educated, that is for sure, but you started telling us things that she did, and we concluded her lack of experience was causing some ills. On more than occasion, your mom and I had a conference up at the school to solve the dilemma at hand. That did change some things, but it was never "just right." We never completely liked that young lady or how she taught you at all. Eventually, this problem came to an end. When your mom and I split up, she moved to Plano which had excellent schools. Something bad turned into something good, at least for you and your time at school. Harrington Elementary, over there, was a very good school and I do not remember having issues with your teachers there. They were talented and you learned even more.

That shows us, as I hint above, that sometimes something trying in life turns into something good. The German poet Rainer Maria Rilke, who is a favorite of mine, wrote something like that. One translation says, *"How should we be able to forget those ancient myths that are at the beginning of all peoples, the myths about dragons that at the last moment turn into princesses; perhaps, all the dragons of our lives are princesses, who are only waiting to see us once beautiful and brave. Perhaps everything terrible is in its deepest being something helpless that wants help from us. So... if a sadness rises up before you larger than any you have ever seen, if a restiveness, like light and cloud-shadows, passes over your hands and over all you do, you must think that something is happening with you, that life has not forgotten you, that it holds you in its hand; it will not let you fall."*

Certainly, some bad teachers in your life gave way to those who were beautiful and brave. So maybe Rilke is right on these things. In your case, it is for sure so remember that when things get tough "life…will not let you fall".

PSE, Marsha, and Roger

To Roger:

All of us have heard or experienced horror stories about preschool day care in our modern world. You can turn on the news or listen to a friend and hear tales describing rotten caregivers, bad food for the kids, or legions of sick and dirty kids.

All in all such things are common in our modern world. But sometimes, there is a bright and wonderful exception to these commonly seen woes. One exception to this perceived rule of thumb was Pre School Enrichment, PSE for short, and the wonderful lady who owned it named Ms. Marsha Clark.

Before your sister was born, we took you up to PSE, based on a recommendation we had received. It was, and still is, in North Richland Hills on Chapman Road, just a few miles from where I live. Back then, we would drive up 820, then Davis, and onto Chapman we would go. PSE was in a red brick building with a chain link fenced around its yard. Swing sets were strewn around the grass, and few shade trees were on the side. It was not your typical chain or franchise type of place. It had a safe and welcome feel, one that made you feel at home in fact. That sense of good extended far inside of its walls because the staff and their ways were one source of that common good. The ultimate source of that well-being was Marsha herself. I don't remember her degrees or licenses or the like, but I remember how she dealt with your mom and me, and most importantly you. She knew about preemies so there was never a concern that you would not receive the care you should.

She and her staff worked with you individually each day and you always seemed to like it there. Marsha would report back on how you were doing and described your progress and how you acted. She said you were a good and happy little boy who learned fast as well. As time went on, we saw you grow and improve. Your developmental problems, due to your early birth, were seen less and less over time.

PSE was more than just playtime; it was medicine for you as well. Because of that, I can truly say placing you there was one of the best things me and your mom decided to do with you. I still feel that way now seeing you grown.

After a while, you left PSE and went into kindergarten. Sycamore school and Mrs. Travis were the next things to move you down school's long diploma road. But I can never forget PSE, even after more than twenty years. Sometimes when I go home, I go up Davis and cut across North Richland Hills to my house in Fort Worth. I go by Chapman, and there is PSE, looking the same as it always has; a little red schoolhouse with kids and cars around it each day. I can still picture us there and see Marsha, who was a very nice-looking lady, too, in my mind.

It would be safe to say she still helps many little kids at PSE, **enriching** their lives as she did for you. She did more than teach you, she ***enriched*** you in many ways. So when you look into the mirror now, remember her and PSE because they helped make you the young man you are today.

Jeffery W. Turner

Playing Sports

To Roger and Jane:

Most kids play some sport growing up. Some kids are good athletes, and some are not. Kids like one sport but not another. Some don't play one at all. You guys played sports, and this is that tale.

Roger played only one sport, which was pee-wee football. Like me, you were not a good athlete and did not like it much. I remember going to your practices and games and seeing you in your uniform, helmet, and pads. Since you weren't that good, you seldom got to play. You never said much about that, but I knew how that felt because I had been the same way even when I was on the high school varsity team. Blocking and chucking a pigskin were not natural things for you to do, much less enjoy. So you did not play another sport again. I too, quit one sport–basketball–in the middle of my second season in fifth grade, so I know how that feels too.

Now Jane, you took more after your mom and my dad who had some athletic ability. You played soccer as a goalie and then softball in high school as well. You had some natural ability to be out on a pitch or a ball field, and you liked it too. Like with Roger's games, I remember the drives to Plano or The Colony to see yours.

Sometimes, you both lost, and sometimes, both of you won. That is the nature of sports, regardless of how you played them or your level of skill. Even so, the benefits of playing a sport go beyond merely playing it to victory or not. Being on a team and putting up with adversity to make yourself better are things that you will always need on a job or raising family. Knowing how to work with others and run a project comes from what you did on the field. Remembering the playbook and everyone's position is like managing a team when you are off of the field. The principals are really the same.

Jeffery W. Turner

So next time the lights go on in the stadium of your life and the game is on think back to what you learned on your own "field of dreams" now gone.

Feeding You Solid Food

To Roger and Jane:

One major milestone on babies' journeys to "toddlerhood" is when they start eating solid food and put away the bottle. It is not an instantaneous process and is one that is messy as well. You kids were just as messy as any babies, and there was no real difference in what each of you did.

The first thing parents try to get their little ones to eat is hot cereal. Some Gerber junk out of a box you cook like oatmeal or grits. One adds some sugar or butter to make it tastier. After putting the baby in the highchair and affixing a bib the real fun begins.

With each of you, we got a little baby spoon, maybe one the little silver ones we got as gifts, and scooped up a tiny portion of the warm gruel from the bowl. Then we gently tried to get it in your toothless and drooling mouth, so you could have a taste. This was not always successful because you would refuse to open up, somehow smear it on your face, or spit it all over your bib, the high chair, or us, too. However after numerous attempts, the light bulb went on, and you accepted and liked the warm mush being proffered up. But the mess remained because even if you liked it, a bunch of it wound up in places other than your mouths. Sometimes, you would deliberately spit it out with a fiendish smile and a grin on your face.

The next progression was to go to baby food. More stuff from Gerber, but this time the formless goo was in a jar. By that time, you understood the process and would open your mouth to receive it. But then the next problem would ensue that foreshadowed your later adult tastes in food. That was finding out which flavor you would like enough to eat. I use the word flavor loosely because the few times I forced myself to taste the so-called food, it was horrific at best. I guess as an infant you just don't know any better and like it anyway. Regardless, after some trial and error, we found the ones you liked and would regularly eat.

The mashed-up green peas, resembling the "Green Slime" from a cheesy sci-fi flick from the 70s, was not one of them. But macaroni and cheese was one for example.

With the eating of solid food attained, one might think the parents' problems with baby feeding were over. Not so—then the worst issue arose: massive and messy baby poops. Once consuming the Gerber stuff or some other food we prepared like that, your diapers were soon filled with huge and disgusting fecal massifs. Sometimes, the poop oozed out of your diapers and onto your clothes. Sometimes so much and so bad, we had to bathe you in the tub—not to mention the clothes going into the washer too. While we were gagging at the smell and cleaning you off, there was one small consolation at least for me. That small bit of relief was the many jokes I made about the poop being bean dip, chili, or guacamole. This made your mom ill and ill-disposed to me for which I paid a dear price.

One time, I made some smart aleck remark about one of Roger's large and hideous poops. Your mom got me back in a most creative way. I remember driving down I-30 to downtown and smelling something funny. I pulled over when I was close to Riverside and pulled out my lunch sack. Well, you guessed it. No turkey sandwich was inside, but a very dirty diaper was in my lunch sack in all of its putrid glory. Touché: your mom got me back in a most creative way. I had to buy my lunch that day too obviously.

After many months, you would finally eat normal food, and once potty trained, this nightmare was concluded. But as you can see, even with the process being so trying and many times messy—if not outright sickening—there was still something to laugh about. Remembering that stinky diaper stuffed in my lunch bag, the seemingly endless boxes of handy wipes, and holding my breath so I wouldn't puke is forever worth the agony I felt at the time.

Jane the Geologist

To Jane:

All kids get interested in a hobby or past time as they grow up. It can be something unexpected, something that they see on TV, or an interest they see a parent enjoy. In your case, you got interested in rocks and fossils, perhaps from hearing me talk about geology and the oil business, which I knew a bit about.

You got the rock bug before Christmas one year and I did some research on what to buy to get you started on that. I bought you two books: *Roadside Geology of Texas* and *A Field Guide to Fossils of Texas*. The first book had road routes you could take through different areas of the state which highlighted the rock formations along the way. The other described the fossils you might find in a location or in a rock. Needing more than books, I found you a real rock hammer and magnifying glass. With books and tools in hand, we went rock and fossil hunting on weekends when you were with me.

On one, we went down Highway 180 from Mineral Wells, looking at the Cretaceous limestone that lined the way. We stopped at spots noted in the books and got out of my truck and hammered away. We did something like that on 377, north of Granbury too, in the road cuts there—limestone again, in fact. But the real find was not there and was seen on an expedition down Fall Creek near Acton.

Dinosaur Park near Glen Rose is a place where the bed of the Brazos River has exposed tracks of the ancient reptiles from the distant past. You can walk by them and see their footprints and toes, sometimes their claws as well. That same limestone was in the Fall Creek area and made up its bed. One Saturday, we went walking down Fall Creek, west of the bridge, and found a track in the rock that was not covered with water. I had a camera with me and took some shots. A picture of it is still in a frame on your desk at my house. You can see the three pointy toes in the white limestone surrounding it. Something big and hungry had walked that way millions of years before.

As time went on, the track disappeared. Once, not so many years ago, I tried to find it and had no luck at all. I found out that many times the rock is fragile, and tracks don't last long sometimes. Like the beast that made the print, the track was washed away by the endless waters of time flowing down the creek.

After some time, you lost interest in this hobby and turned to other things. Kids are like that, as are adults. Interests come and go as the years go by. Some remain throughout life. Even though rocks aren't your thing now, I can see the same spark in your eyes with the animals you study at college. Do you remember when I came to Galveston, and we went to the marsh where you and your class had tagged the hermit crabs? When you were poking around in the water and mud, I saw not just you as twenty years old in college, but also you at Fall Creek that day. The times looking at rocks are like the footprints the dinosaurs left in the limestone and are like tracks in the riverbed of time.

Jeffery W. Turner

They make a mark, are seen for a while, and then disappear because nothing lasts forever. But while we are here, the footprints are there for us to see and be reminded of the steps we, and those before us, took down the fast stream of being alive.

Notes To My Kids: Little Stories About Grown Up Kids

Roger the Rifleman

To Roger:

When I was a kid, Granddad Tom took me dove and quail hunting on some family member's farm. When I was small and did not have a gun, he made we walk behind him and check where I was at all times. He did that to keep me safe and teach me where not be when a group is hunting. When I was older and got my first gun, he always asked if it, a Daisy BB gun, was on safety or not. Later when I got my first shotgun, an Ithaca .20 gauge, the lessons continued unabated as before, each time he asked if my gun was on safety or not. With your granddad, safety was first before marksmanship or making a shot. He was never the type that went out in the country and "shot everything that moved," like some people we knew did. Those lessons paid off. None of us were ever hurt or got shot because of the strict safety drill he taught. Those lessons stayed with me. When you wanted a gun, I continued his ways.

One Christmas, I decided to get you a .22 rifle instead of a shotgun. Why you ask? Well, after my BB gun, your granddad had me practice on his .22. What was good enough for Granddad and I was good enough for you and me I thought. I went to Wal-Mart and bought the gun, which was placed under the tree along with ammo for it, too. When you opened it up, you were very excited to see it, a real gun in your midst—I remember the Christmas when I got my shotgun and was excited just the same.

Since we did not have a farm to go shoot at, we went to the gun range at Whiskey Flats to teach you to shoot. I showed you how to load the gun and most importantly where the safety was. Just like my dad, I started the endless process of asking if your gun was on safety and telling you how to handle it. I explained why I was doing that; you were perhaps a little irritated at the endless safety quiz; hence you were just like me when I was young. I knew why Granddad asked what he did, but every 20 seconds? Yes, the question was asked frequently to get you into the habit of being aware of the gun's safety and what it was set on. You learned to shoot okay at the range, too. In the end, you became Roger the Rifleman in my mind.

As you grew up, you retained an interest in guns. Not the shotguns and rifles your granddad and I had—but handguns, which were more to your liking. Now you have a CHL and own a handgun or two. I don't know if your original .22 sparked this interest, but it at least continues the practice of shooting guns in the family. Therefore, it seems that Roger the Rifleman has become Roger the Grown-up Handgun Owner, who shoots at the range. So when you pick up your gun at the range and slip in a clip, check your safety and always remember me asking you if it was on at the Whiskey Flats range. And rest assured, my son, I can still hear *my* dad asking me the same simple question when I was young: "***Is your safety on?***"

Jeffery W. Turner

Trick or Treat with an Assault Rifle

To Roger and Jane:

When we lived on Monterrey Drive, your mom and I would take you two up and down the street on Halloween for trick-or-treat. We would dress you up in whatever costume you had that year, and one of us would take you out, while the other stayed at the house to hand out candy to the neighbor kids who knocked on our door. When you moved to Plano, I was not usually part of that process because my visitation seldom fell on All Hallows Eve. Then one Wednesday it did, and I dressed up in costume and went down the street with you, as I had before, but with a rather unique costume and set of equipment.

Most parents who dress up at Halloween and go with their kids down the street normally dress in some tasteful attire that people would expect to see on that night. Not me. To start with, I put on my grey, black, and white urban "camo" battle dress uniform (BDU).

Then I donned my combat boots, black "tactical gloves" (the ones with nothing on the finger tips), and my USMC KA-BAR knife. Atop my head, I put my East German steel "Fritz" helmet and black sunglasses. The real icing to this military costume cake was taking my Russian SKS—the not-so-well-known cousin of the AK-47—assault rifle with me, including a nice banana clip shoved into it. Unloaded, of course, but as you will see, at least one neighbor did not take the joke lightly.

With all of my gear in tow, I got in my truck and drove over to Plano and went to your mom's house. You two were ready to go and were dressed up. You kids were quite amazed at the sight of me and thought it was neat to be sure. You picked up your bags for the goodies, we went out your front door, and started down the street. You would go up to a door and ring the doorbell. I stood behind you at first. Then someone would open the door, and you said, "Trick or treat," with great enthusiasm and a smile, and promptly received your treats. That was the typical part of the drill; but when the home owner saw me, the real treat—err, trick—was to be had.

Most people thought it was neat and made some funny remark to me, which was good. You kids giggled or laughed, too. At some homes, I said something like, "Give my kids ALL of your candy … or else," after you said trick or treat nicely, of course. That continued, as we went down the streets around your house. But then one neighbor did not see the humor in our method of obtaining candy as you will recall.

The next day I called you and one of you told me that a soccer mom was not well disposed to my costume and had called the police out of alarm; a false alarm of course, since my gun was not loaded. A paranoid, do-gooder soccer mom did not think it was "appropriate" for me to walk around her precious neighborhood with a gun around kids. Even a firearm with no rounds in it at that—unbelievable was it not? Some people have no sense of humor it seems. Oh well, her loss, I say.

Lest we forget that evening, I have a picture of us in our scary gear at my house taken that night. You two are at my side smiling with big, happy grins and me in the middle, hoisting up the gun for all to see. Regardless of the soundness of my chosen attire, it was a fun and memorable night with you.

Coming back to the present day and looking back, perhaps I did err by carrying the SKS with me. Yes, an SKS, not an AK-47, remember. Why? Folks who do not know one gun from another do not know the difference from an SKS and an AK-47, and in the case of the falsely terrified soccer mom and those like her, their rear ends.

Life is like that you see. You two got a huge kick out of me and my garb that night, and we had a load of fun. But that lady who called the cops did not see it that way. You can do something with gleeful innocence, but have it viewed with alarm by others. Hence, what you think is a treat may turn out to be a trick, even when it's not Halloween.

Jeffery W. Turner

A Baby Doll for Jane

To Jane:

All little girls love baby dolls, and you were no different. From when you were a baby to your preteens, you had an army of dolls and later Barbies that filled your closets. Still do, I might add, seeing the box filled with Barbies in your room at my house. These little likenesses of kids, babies, and moms came from many stores, but one of them came from a store that was more than a cookie cutter Toys "R" Us or discount store. Instead, the source of it was a magical little doll store near our old house on Monterrey Drive in the Handley area.

On a stretch of Lancaster, a few old buildings had been restored and were filled with small businesses. One of them was Enchanted Dolls. I do not know how we found out about it, but I took you there to look a few times. We would drive down Handley, swing onto Lancaster, go past the Red Rooster lumber yard that Granddad Tom liked to shop at, and park in front of the store. We would go inside and would be in a different world. That world was one of fine, custom-made dolls and not the ones that were made by the millions overseas that flooded the look-alike stores. These dolls were sometimes very expensive. Being little, the price was not your care, but the huge array of these sometimes lifelike dolls was. You walked around the store in wide-eyed silence, tugging at their clothes, stroking their hair, and holding them too. The lady that ran the store was obviously enthralled by your interest. Of course, she wanted to sell some dolls and helped you try to find the perfect baby doll.

You mom took you there, too. On your second birthday, you got a fine doll from there. It was not cheap, nor was it the most expensive, and looked like a real baby girl in appearance. You named her Alice and she became your favorite doll. You dearly loved and adored Alice and played with her so much MeeMaw had to sew her back together at least once.

Like all of your dolls, you treated Alice like a real child when it was in your little arms. You would play like she was getting a bottle and tried to make her burp, or you would sing her a lullaby. These simple actions imitated life and time went on around these playful actions as you got older. And get older you did and finally stopped playing with your dolls, having outgrown them for sports and boys.

Since Alice from Enchanted Dolls is not at my house, I assume she is at your mom's in a box or maybe standing in a corner staring at your now empty room. Regardless of where she and your other dolls now lie, they are an allegory of life in a way. As I said above, you played like you fed and cared for Alice and her fellow doll-mates and that play taught you how to care for a real baby of your own. Maybe that is why girls are more natural with babies than boys sometimes. The boys play sports or army but not with dolls when they are little. Of course, what boys play with teaches them other things that are just as important and valuable too,— things a man shows a boy to be a good man. But the doll play, again, shows a little girl what to do with an infant when she is a mom. Hence, that little doll named Alice from Enchanted Dolls cast a magical spell on you, one that will make you a better mom simply by having cared for it as you did so innocently and so lovingly, so long ago.

Jeffery W. Turner

Time's a Funny Thing

To Roger and Jane:

When you two were small children, the movie *Always* came out. It still is one of my personal favorites. In it, Pete, an air tanker pilot played by Richard Dreyfuss, gets killed in an accident. In the afterlife, his guardian angel, Hap played by Audrey Hepburn, tries to guide him to final peace and acceptance of his fate.

In one scene, Pete and Hap travel back and forth in time, seeing his past. While they sit in some forest, Hap tells the **temporally** confused Pete, "Time's a funny thing." Indeed, it is. I think you'll see below.

During the Christmas holidays Roger came over to see me the day you went back to Galveston Jane. On New Year's Eve Day, we went to eat at a Russian restaurant in Arlington. On the way, we went through east Fort Worth, where we used to live. In a short time, we went back and forth in time like Pete did in the movie.

After going down Loop 820, we exited at Brentwood Stair Road. We drove down Brentwood past the Kolache Shop, Little Tykes day care, and the bank building where your mom once worked. As we drove down Brentwood, we talked about Best Mart—the convenience store a little north of there we always used for gas, beer, and snacks when we went to the New Park. We spent a lot of time at its playground or looking at the horses in the pasture next to it. The horses are no longer there; the pasture they once grazed in is now a field of houses.

We turned down Sandy Lane and around us were the 1960's era brick veneer homes surrounded by oak trees, which looked much like they did when we lived there. Then we took a left onto Monterrey Drive to see the old house itself. Similar to what we saw on Sandy, the houses seemed to be the same. Memories surfaced as we drove past the homes of our former neighbors, like the Simpsons, the Jeffries—whose kids you played with—or Mrs. Shaw who was always in a bad mood.

And then we were in front of the old house itself. The big trees were still there, bigger than before, but the house was mostly the same. The dormers still looked out over the front yard from your old rooms upstairs, and the big tree in the middle of the back still cast its branches over the yard. The big bay window by the front door also looked the same: how many times did we peer out its frames to see what was outside? The owners had painted the red brick a medium gray, but that was the only obvious change. And next to it was Jess and Madge's old house which really did look unchanged. At that moment, I could see us there with Jess on a warm summer day. A grandfather, he would smile at you two and ask what you had been doing at school. Such things happened over 20 years ago, but it seemed like we were still there as if time had stood still.

Coming back to the present, we turned around and went further down Sandy, and there was the Old Park. The playground equipment that you two once scurried over was replaced long ago with newer stuff. But the trees remained, along with the ball field, and at the north end of the park was our old back yard fence. The second story of the house and the big tree on the back property line still looked above its top. The year could have been 1985, 1995 or 2005, and it would have looked the same.

Next, we continued south on Sandy and drove past the cemetery where Lee Harvey Oswald lies in his unmarked grave. Nothing much had changed. The same houses, buildings, and trees still stood guard along the street where they had always been.

 We drove on to Arlington and turned on to Lancaster to the east, beside the railroad tracks going past unchanged areas of trees and pastures. About the only new things were the gas wells in the fields. The leafless, but timeless, post oaks were still there reaching quietly upward around the new wellheads and tanks.

When we got into Arlington, we drove past the Campo Verde restaurant where we used to eat. I wondered if the food was as good as it was in the past. On the outside it looked the same as if nearly twenty years hadn't passed. As we neared the Russian place, I saw another restaurant we went to: Jo-Ed's Bomber, which made northeastern-style sub sandwiches. It, too, was seemingly unchanged.

After we ate at the Russian place, we went by a house on Bowen Road that your mom and I considered buying. We didn't because it had a foundation leak in the garage. The neighborhood around it, like the old east side, hadn't changed much either. Time had passed but you could not tell that just by driving through the area.

That day was a trip down Memory Lane seeing what had been the fabric of our lives. On the way to eat lunch, we saw a big slice of our past in just a couple of hours. Just as Pete saw his life go back and forth before his eyes in that short scene in *Always,* we saw a big part of our lives go by as we drove down those once frequently traveled roads.

So Hap was right you see, time *is* a funny thing. Things and places change and sometimes they don't, even though *decades* have flown past. What *was* still *is,* even though the world and time has moved on at least in our memories. Hence, they should not be forgotten and should be tucked away in our hearts and minds to be revisited from time to time. When we go back to our old haunts, we see where we came from and recall important events from our lives once more.

Maybe that is why I write. In a way, recording the past helps us make drives like we did that day. The written remembrances are a trip down memory's long interstate highway, and recording these events keeps them from fading away in our rear-view mirrors. Hence, our family will keep going down time's long road by you recalling the tales in this book. Hopefully one day, by your own extended families and kids. Then one day you can tell them *time's a funny thing* too, just like Hap told Pete.

Afterward

The third book in the *Notes* series is now done. I hope the stories gave you something to remember about your own children.

The mixture of good times and bad times with kids is par for the course when raising them. It is a time in life that is filled with many things that will both make you happy and also sadden and haunt you in your older years.

Regardless, it is a story most of us have been a character in. It is a natural thing to have children and to tell them, or their offspring, these stories. In that, may be the true value of what I have written. Retelling events of a family, its stories, and describing the members of its generations is a worthwhile thing. It is part of what makes us whom we are and tells us about what we are made of as human beings.

Now you may be curious about my next *Notes* book. The next one will be *Notes About My Family*. This book will be stories about my childhood and growing up. There will be stories about my mom and dad (you heard some of them here), my grandparents, and other members of my extended family. Tales from oil well blowouts and seeing Apollo 11 blast off when I was nine to picnics at the farm near Valley View, Texas will be told. I hope you'll like them, too. There may be a fifth book too—a compendium of *Notes* on any and everything, some of which I have already written.

Jeffery W. Turner, 10/27/2012

Thanks To & Pictures

More than one person has made this book possible. In no particular order and with ***great*** thanks:

Elaine, for book formatting.

Margo, for copy editing.

Ruby, Jeff "B", and the Keller Fort Worth Writers Group, for editing, support, and comment.

And

MeeMaw, "Roger," and "Jane," of course–I love you all.

Cover pictures: family pictures of me and the kids "Jane" had. Cover: my mom and dad's house by the pool. Back: the Monterrey house.

For More Information

My book website:

www.ilypants.net

Links to my blog, Facebook page, and other things.

My website for photographs I take:

http://www.redbubble.com/people/jeffturnerphoto/

www.ingramcontent.com/pod-product-compliance
Lightning Source LLC
Chambersburg PA
CBHW060109170426
43198CB00010B/824